Corporate Cash Management

Corporate Cash Management

PHILIPPA L. BACK

WOODHEAD-FAULKNER · CAMBRIDGE

Published in Great Britain by Woodhead-Faulkner Ltd
Fitzwilliam House, 32 Trumpington Street, Cambridge CB2 1QY, England

Published in the United States of America by
Nichols Publishing Company, PO Box 96,
New York, NY 10024, USA

First published 1988

British Library Cataloguing in Publication Data

Back, Philippa L.
Corporate cash management.
1. Business enterprises—Finance
I. Title
658.1'5 HG4026

ISBN 0-85941-390-x

Library of Congress Cataloging in Publication Data

Back, Philippa.
Corporate cash management/Philippa L. Back.
p. cm.
ISBN 0-89397-294-0
1. Corporations—Cash position. 2. Cash management. I. Title.
HG4028.C45B29 1988
658.1'5244—dc19 87-25946
CIP

Designed by Geoff Green

Typeset by Wyvern Typesetting Ltd, Bristol

Printed in Great Britain by
St Edmundsbury Press Ltd, Bury St Edmunds, Suffolk

Contents

INTRODUCTION

What is corporate cash management? The simple answer is that it is the management of the company's cash resources. However, in a world of ever-changing circumstances this simplicity belies the importance of the function.

The cash management function is not an isolated one. Thus the concept of the organisation structure, its ethos and objectives must be appreciated and understood prior to defining the requirements of the function itself. These are explained in Chapters 1 and 2.

In interfacing with other line control functions, it relies heavily on the information fed into it to ensure its own efficiency. The nature of information flows will be reviewed in Chapter 3, and manipulation into forecasts in Chapters 4 and 5.

This aspect of interdependence through information flow cannot be stressed too highly in the practical running of the cash management department. Information on the timing of cash requirements and surpluses, or more particularly changes to previous foreseen timings, can severely alter the risk profile of an organisation in a given situation. This is irrespective of the size of the organisation or amount involved since relevancy will operate. To a large multinational a million of currency may be 'insignificant' but to the operating unit where that million arises the significance is plain. In reality this significance and concern should be reflected at multinational level, though as a practical issue this will largely depend on the structure of the organisation.

'Situations', or exposures are identified through the process of collating information; these need to be managed (Chapter 5).

In conceptual terms the strength of the cash flow within a company is a better indicator of the health of that company than the value of its balance sheet. It is that cash flow therefore that must be managed effectively and efficiently; hence the need for a 'cash management function'. In Chapter 6 the issue of managing the inherent exposure within the cash cycle is examined in more detail; but as an indication of the above, the company whose payables are on 30 days net and receivables on 60 days net will, in crude terms, have a 30-day financing problem within the cash cycle. Some measures can be taken to lessen the risk that this position presents if it cannot be improved by renegotiating the terms of purchases and sales. The risk needs to be monitored, in conjunction with the credit controller monitoring poor payers and bad debts.

Chapters 7 and 8 seek specifically to identify the different ways of managing interest rate and currency exposures by detailing the workings of the money market and the instruments traded in them.

Since the cash management function plays a key role it is important that tight controls are enforced on its operation. These are to ensure the function is run within the overall objectives of the organisation and the parameters set on the department itself. Such control features will be discussed in Chapter 9.

The classification and importance of the function these days are a feature of the human and financial resources that are attributed to it. Some of these will be reviewed in Chapter 10, including the circular debate of whether the cash management function should be regarded as a profit centre.

In large corporations the department will tend to fall within a designated treasury function. This function will likely encompass longer-term aspects of financial planning, such as corporate finance or capital markets activities. None of these aspects can be managed in isolation. All long-term financings become short in the sense that as the rollover date nears, a decision has to be made about the next interest period. Similarly, interest due (or receivable) has to be paid or collected, normally the concern of the cash management department as the purveyors of short-term cash. If, in these larger companies, the cash area is not directly involved, it will be or should be by virtue of the information flow on the foreseen changes in the bank balances it monitors. On this scale the allocated resources will be extensive, both in terms of dedicated, professional personnel responsible for individual aspects of the company's financial picture and in terms of technological back-up. The latter might be electronic banking services, database information retrieval systems, and computerised recording and monitoring of the company's financial position. In a smaller company the situation is likely to be different.

In a sense it is difficult to draw a comparison on resource allocation to cash management since it does not depend on the overall size of the company concerned. It is more a feature of the type of company and the trade it transacts. For instance, a large sole trade construction company may run a cash department on resources similar to those of a small freight forwarding company. In the former case, contracts are of a longer-term nature and the day-to-day requirements are those of ensuring the company's financial obligations are met. In the latter case, however, the flow of cash is crucial to the smooth operation of the company as a whole, since goods cannot be shipped or released unless funds have been passed.

The summary (Chapter 11) emphasises the theme of the book that exposures need to be identified, assessed, actioned and monitored within the context of the organisation's objectives.

As background to the different methods of covering exposures, an Appendix on the banking systems in the major countries has been included.

Corporate Cash Management will give practical assistance to those companies establishing or setting up a treasury function, whose first stage is often most readily and easily identified as a cash management department. The book, therefore, has relevance to corporate managements representing all sizes of companies. In addition, it will give an insight to those involved in the advisory and consultancy fields in this specialised area of the finance function.

CHAPTER 1

Organisational Structure

CHAPTER AIM

To appreciate how company organisational structures will affect the efficiencies of financial risk management; to understand the role of the finance function.

In setting up a designated cash management function, it is important to view its role within the context of the company's overall management structure – in particular the chain of decision-making. Financial markets are volatile and decisions must be made on a continuing basis. The results of these decisions can have far-reaching implications for the company and its financial performance.

STRUCTURE TYPES

Organisational structures will vary from company to company. They develop as a result of combining historical precedent and personal character. Companies tend only rarely to go through step changes with regard to organisation and management, although the structure provides the framework. This is because the quality and nature of management decisions are influenced by the nature of the organisation itself.

An organisation has two facets, one formal and one informal, both relating to the network of communications within the company. The formal part is laid down in company rules, and in the required exchange of information between members of the company. To be effective, it requires willingness to communicate. The informal part rests more on the individuals or subcompany within a group who, due to lack of clarity or misunderstanding of the formal rules, will react independently. This can be beneficial or detrimental to the organisation as a whole. Figures 1.1–1.4

provide illustrations of formal and informal company and management organisation.

Informal communications and information flow are usually a useful

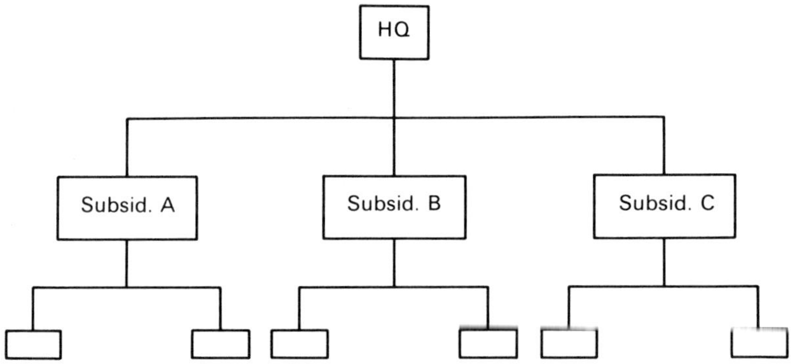

Fig. 1.1 Formal company organisation.

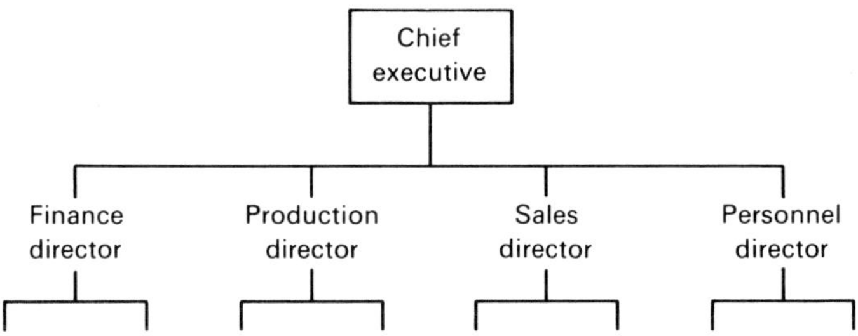

Fig. 1.2 Formal management organisation.

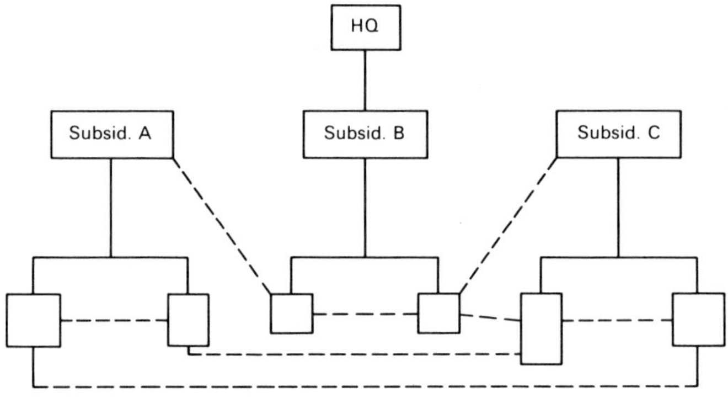

Fig. 1.3 Informal company organisation: the dotted line relationships.

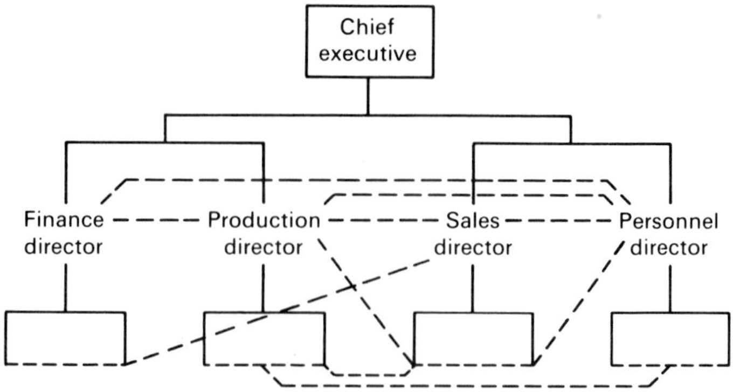

Fig. 1.4 Informal management organisation: the dotted line relationships.

adjunct to the formal systems. However, there is always a danger in the hierarchical pyramid management arrangement that the headquarters or chief executive may become remote or isolated.

Organisations typically consist of line relationships, with each level reporting to the person directly above. In addition, companies may base their structures on functional, geographical or product reporting relationships, or on a combination as in a matrix organisation.

As stated earlier, each company's structure is individual and largely predicated by its growth and management philosophies over time.

A simplified company growth profile could be represented as in Fig. 1.5.

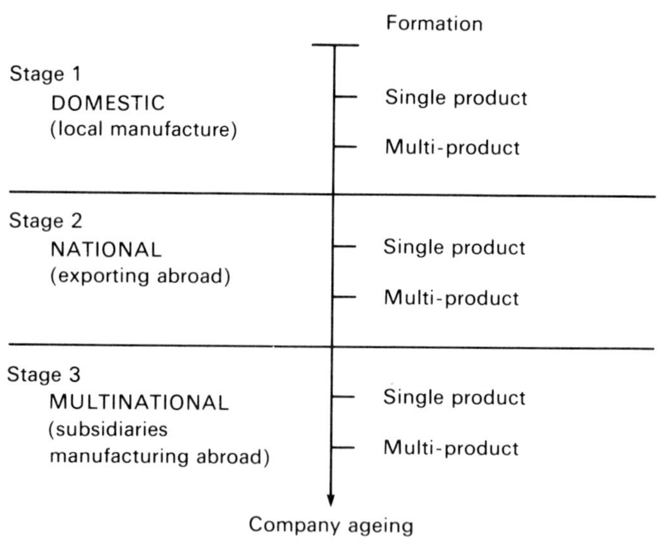

Fig. 1.5 Company growth profile.

As a generalisation, at each stage the company's structure would evolve and develop, from probably being entrepreneurially based initially to being led by a management team at the multinational stage. During the process of evolution the emphasis will have swung from production to sales, marketing and so forth as guiding forces. However, throughout each stage, and in increasing importance as the company structure grows more complicated, there is the finance function.

FINANCE FUNCTION

The finance function has a strategic role to play. Its structure will vary but in a multinational will tend to be organised as in Fig. 1.6.

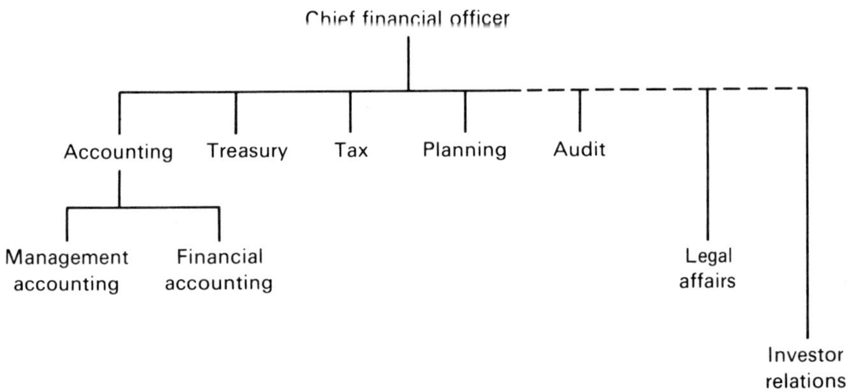

Fig. 1.6 Structure of the finance function.

Audit, legal affairs and investor relations departments are often seen as distinct from the finance function, but allied to it; hence the dotted line relationship. Audit is often kept separate as a control feature.

ROLE

The combined role of the departments is to provide finance for the commercial business and support its operations, capital investment and growth. This is achieved firstly by recording and collating the state of the business through the management accounting process. Secondly, the information is analysed. This analysis is likely to be carried out by each department using its expertise in the relevant manner.

The analysis will be broadly based on monitoring ratios over time, comparing these with budget targets and strategic plans. The particular performances looked at can be those measured on absolute values, usually profitability criteria of some sort, or on relative values, i.e. the return on investment or capital employed.

Profitability criteria

Profit can be defined in a number of ways when used as a performance measure of subsidiaries. In theory, only those factors which are within the local management's control should be included in profit (i.e. controllable profit). These would include variable items of costs and revenue such as sales income, cost of labour, materials, and short-term interest charges relating to locally run working capital items such as debtors and stocks. Fixed overheads, which again are controllable locally, should be included, e.g. advertising, administrative and supervisory costs.

Where costs are allocated to a subsidiary, such as management charges from central administration or computer costs from a shared user, they should not be included since local management by definition has no control over them. This is true also where central policy dictates investment/disinvestment policies and depreciation charges. Again, if local management can control these factors then they should be included.

A refinement of the above is called controlled residual profit, which is sales revenue less controllable subsidiary costs (as above) and interest, imputed on the investment in the subsidiary by the parent. The latter element is an additional factor over controllable profit. In this instance depreciation would be charged on the fixed assets, and the imputed interest charge would be on the amount invested at the company's (the group's) cost of capital.

In using profitability measures it must be decided whether the profit will be on an after-tax or pre-tax basis. In many group companies there is an election for group relief for tax purposes, which will affect the amount of tax paid overall. However, against this a subsidiary in a particular location may be 'profitable' by its taking advantage of local tax investment and allowance schemes. The decision is a complex one, though in general companies will use a before-tax measure.

The profitability measure will be looked at relative to budget and plan, and compared in percentage terms from reporting cycle to reporting cycle (typically monthly).

Relative criteria

The most commonly used measure is return on capital employed (ROCE) or its alternative, return on investment (ROI).

The basic formula for ROCE is:

$$\text{ROCE} = \frac{\text{Profit}}{\text{Capital employed (or investment)}} \times 100\%$$

In the pyramid of ratios, as generally referred to in this topic of ratio analysis, the component parts of the ratio are:

$$\text{ROCE} = \frac{\text{Sales}}{\text{Capital employed (or investment)}} \times \frac{\text{Profit}}{\text{Sales}} \times 100\%$$

This measure has real value only where local management has control over both profit and investment in the local subsidiary, as in the controlled residual profit calculation.

The profit element of the formula would be calculated as in the preceding section. However, several different bases can be used to define capital employed or investment. It should be realised that bias from accounting procedures can mask the underlying levels of operational efficiency. In an instance where original cost is used as a base, a subsidiary with older assets will show better ratios that one with newer plant and equipment. There are three basic valuation methods commonly based on average values for the year, and not year-end values.

1. Gross book value: When an asset is replaced its book value will increase by the difference between the original cost of the old asset and the cost of the new. However, the relevant capital cost is the cost of the new less the sale price of the old. Since in many instances the sale price of the old asset will be below its original cost, the capital cost of the new asset will be understated using gross book value, as follows:

Description	Old asset	New asset
Cost as new	100,000	150,000
Book value after 5 years (reducing balance depreciation at 10% p.a.)	59,049	
Sale value	35,000	
Gross book value of asset = cost of new − original cost of old = 50,000		
Relevant capital cost = new asset − sale value = 115,000		
Understatement of capital cost of new asset = 115,000 − 50,000 = 65,000		

2. Net book value: This will show an increase in rate of return as each period the capital assets value is written down by depreciation. In this instance an improving ROCE might be in conflict with reducing profits.
3. Current replacement cost: This is a measure of valuing assets according to their opportunity costs or economic value to the

business. It is the most theoretically apt of the three instances, though it can be difficult to measure.

Using the above ratios the company can set targets for all its subsidiaries, against which they will be monitored. While ROCE and profitability measures are useful summaries, no single measure can take account of the various influences on subsidiaries; thus a range of objectives should be set, covering sales, market share, growth, productivity and so forth.

As previously stated, the finance function will review the figures against the pre-set targets and objectives. The reaction to the results of the review obviously depends on the areas of weakness found. Management accounting tends to be a monthly cycle, so any deterioration is soon brought to the attention of senior management.

The finance function will look particularly at growth in pre-interest trading profits, cash flow generation (in amount and volatility) and the ROCE. These will be reviewed in the context of the group's ratios, its growth and earnings per share and dividends per share, quality and volatility of earnings, and the overall return on equity.

In addition to measuring and monitoring, the finance function will normally be responsible for resource allocation. This entails the evaluation of capital expenditure, acquisitions and disposals, and recommendation of a dividend policy in line with the company's targets. The evaluation is in financial terms, leaving the commercial aspects of the project in question to be assessed by general management – although an understanding of commercial logic is essential in the evaluation.

The ultimate responsibility of the finance function is to ensure the company has sufficient (or access to sufficient) financial resources to continue in business. This is typically delegated to the treasury or cash management department (see Chapter 2).

CENTRALISATION V. DECENTRALISATION

Financial management can be decentralised or centralised, or a combination of the two. Again, the optimum solution will be prejudiced by the type of company and the state of its evolution (see Fig. 1.5).

Domestic, single product

In the first stages of development, a company will be highly centralised. This will reflect the requirements of the founder or founders to be in control. They will be controlling direct, in an entrepreneurial fashion, the production, sales and marketing aspects of the business. Finance too will be centralised, and the financial arrangements simple. The company will deal with a single banker; indeed, personal guarantees may be required from the founder(s) to secure finance for the business. In any event, finance is likely to consist of part equity from the owner and working capital from the bank.

Domestic, multi-product

If the company is operating at a single location the situation will again be highly centralised, in the first instance. If, however, it has grown to be multi-locational there will be elements of delegation. Local site managers will be appointed to oversee production. Purchasing and sales could still be centralised in order to retain the benefits of bulk ordering and customer contact. Finance, like production control, could be delegated in part. A local plant accountant would be appointed, to be responsible for recording activity of the plant in financial terms. A local bank account might be required to facilitate payment of wages and local bills. This may introduce another banker to the organisation.

At some stage the company is likely to begin sourcing its raw materials abroad, requiring financing and currency exposure management.

National, single product

In this instance the company is manufacturing one product, which it sells at home and abroad. Control is likely to be central, though production may be multi-locational. At this stage sales abroad may be direct, but more likely will be through a local agent familiar with the local customers. Sales may be invoiced to the agent in base or local currency. An efficient funds collection service will be required to ensure good value as soon as possible. This may imply multi-banking. In order to receive funds quickly (unless paid direct on open account terms) the company will need a local bank account for the clearing of cheques and drafts. The bank chosen should be a member of the local clearing system and have good correspondent bank links with the lead banker to the company. Such rationality will ensure that funds will be passed swiftly along the chain to the company's own account in the base currency.

National, multi-product

This is similar to the preceding situation, though since there is greater variety there tends to be growing complexity. In this instance more control will likely to have been delegated from the centre in all areas.

The central finance function will monitor funding activity, but the local financial manager will be responsible for raising finance, buying and selling foreign currency, and local banking relationships. This can lead to anomalies in financial control. One subsidiary could be selling currency while another is buying it, and one subsidiary could be borrowing from a bank while another has surplus funds to invest.

Multinational, single product

A multinational company has overseas subsidiaries which manufacture the company's products. The products may be parts, which will be assembled in a single location; or the entire production process, through to a finished product, may be involved. Delegation of responsibility is likely to be more in evidence in the latter example than in the former because if there are problems at the assembly plant, the production plants may have to cut back. This level of integration on a multinational basis needs tight cohesion and monitoring, likely involving the financial control aspects as well. A central finance team will probably monitor the buying and selling of exchange, etc., on behalf of the overseas subsidiaries, subject to local exchange controls and controlled company legislation. In some instances regional treasury centres are set up in tax-favourable locations to ensure the efficient handling of the funds of the multinational.

Where the overseas subsidiary is an integrated one, the finance is likely to be organised at local level. This will again create a multi-bank situation, with subsidiaries setting up their own contacts. The operational difficulties in the group context noted in the preceding section could occur. The system may not be efficient.

Multinational, multi-product

This is the final stage of company growth complexity. Overseas there will be fully integrated operations, sub-holding subsidiaries, cross-border holdings and so forth. At this stage the management structure will likely be highly decentralised in order to retain local management motivation – as well as being the most practical arrangement. Finance will probably be decentralised as well, with the various aspects of the finance function being replicated at the country holding company level. The group will be multi-banked, with a complex network of banking and financing arrangements.

Where local subsidiaries are of sufficient size and strength, decentralised treasury management would tend to be the most efficient if the overall financial scheme is overseen by a central point to ensure no conflicts with group financial policy. If local companies cannot support themselves unsecured, the parent may run their finances for them.

In summary, centralisation or decentralisation is more or less efficient depending on the type of organisation. In management terms the structure can be split geographically, by product or by function. The permutations are endless. Within the finance function, centralisation allows the negotiation of financial resources from a position of greater strength. The centralisation may be on a country or regional basis (there are few instances of a centralised global treasury department). The company is able to monitor currency and interest rate flows, thus optimising them for the best overall return to the group.

Centralisation is also best in terms of rapid decision-making. As pointed out earlier, this is essential with the high volatility of markets. The shorter and clearer the decision tree, the more efficient the overall system.

It is said that centralisation is a demotivator, but it is the degree of centralisation, not the feature itself. It is more important that the organisational structure be well defined; otherwise managers will find it difficult to achieve high performance.

In many companies the optimum situation is decentralised management control with centralised financial control, combined with a monitoring process to oversee local bank contacts – which will always be required.

With either a centralised or decentralised finance function, the need for a specialised team, responsible for the financing of the company, can be identified. At each stage of the company's evolution, new financial demands are put on it – either in having to raise capital for expansion, to exchange base currencies for foreign currencies or to arrange day-to-day functioning of the business. The financial markets are an amalgam of products which need to be assessed and the most suitable ones chosen. This is the role of the specialist, the treasurer (or cash manager).

CHAPTER 2

Objectives

CHAPTER AIM

To appreciate the role of cash management within an organisation; to identify the types of parameters to which the department should adhere; to appreciate the importance of banking relationships.

Once the need for a specialised financial team has been identified, the next stage is to define its scope within the organisation.

The treasury function is a part of the finance function. Its role tends to be broad in relation to the financing, monitoring and controlling of financial resources within a group. The cash management function is a part of treasury. Its role tends to be the handling of cash, the direct interface with the market in buying or selling money or currencies. It implements decisions taken, and acts within guidelines. As a result its view is predominantly short term, versus the long-term strategic financing role that the corporate finance function within treasury plays.

SETTING OBJECTIVES

Before a company identifies the specifics of managing currency or interest rate risk, it needs to set down the broad objectives of the cash management department and ways in which these objectives may be met. Depending on the organisation these objectives may be narrowly or broadly defined, i.e. to include or encompass aspects of broad financial management.

What financial risks are to be managed?

Interest rate risks

These can be the risk of rates rising, where the company's cost of borrowing would increase, or the risk of rates falling, in which case the company that is investing surplus funds would see its returns declining. If the company has a positive attitude to managing interest rate risk, it will require the cash management department to actively manage these potential risks. This management cannot be in isolation: decisions will be made with reference to the budget, the cash flow and the financing plan. These will identify the longer-term profile of the company. The short-term aspect is tied into the working capital cycle (see Chapter 6). Where indications of finance requirements over the shorter horizon are given, decisions will be made with reference to the management accounts.

Currency risks

Currency risks can be identified on three levels:

1. Economic exposure: This is the broadest level of risk exposure. It is the total impact on a company of changes in exchange rates. This exposure is environmental in that it encompasses all the activities of the company at home and abroad. Its effect is economic, a part of business risk, though the implications are financial. Being a broad-brush measure it is difficult to quantify. As a result the risk is split into its component parts of translation and transaction exposure (see Fig. 2.1). This even extends to circumstances where transactional exposure has been covered, that is foreign exchange contracts have been 'booked'.

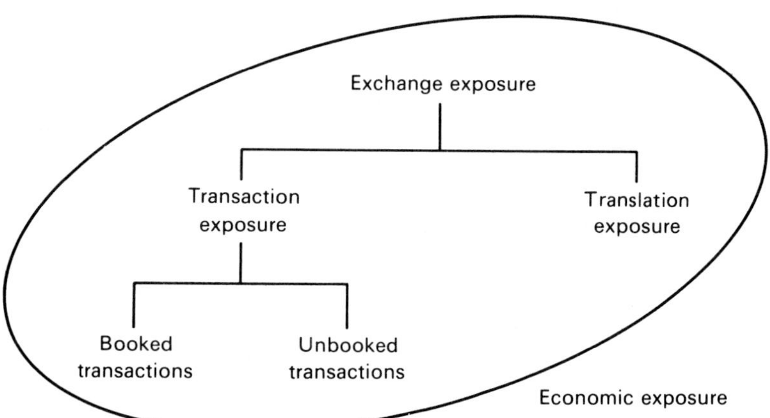

Fig. 2.1 Economic exposure.

2. Translation exposure: This is the effect of changes in currency movements on assets and liabilities in one or more currencies, on consolidation into a base currency at the financial year-end. The quantification and result on a company's balance sheet vary from country to country under different accounting practices. In Fig. 2.2, at

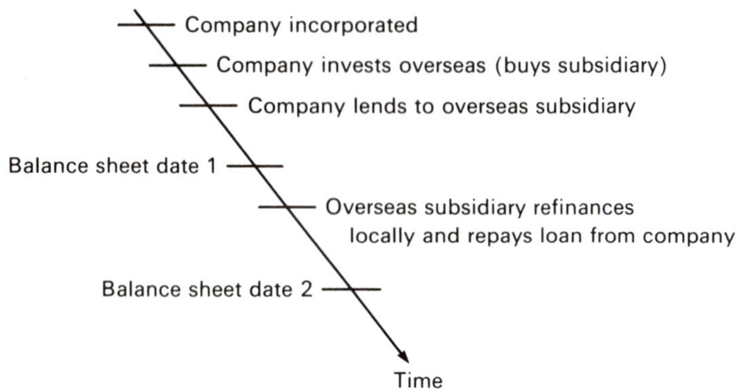

Fig. 2.2 Translation exposure.

balance sheet date 1 the company would revalue its investment and loan (assets) at that date, comparing the revaluation with rates at the time of the acquisition and original loan. At balance sheet date 2 only the investment is outstanding and would be revalued. The exposure usually arises in respect of equity investments or loans (assets) in overseas companies, whether wholly or partly owned. At each balance sheet date the investment would be revalued as previously stated, at the then current exchange rates. If the exchange rate had changed from the previous year-end, which is very likely, the company would show a currency gain or loss accordingly. Unlike other forms of exposure there is not necessarily an end date to translation exposure. With the loan, the end date occurs when it is repaid, although it might be continually renewed. With an equity investment, the end date occurs on the sale of that investment.

3. Transaction exposure: This is the effect of currency movements on current cash flows, and the impact on future flows, between the date of initiating the transaction and its completion (see Fig. 2.3). Transaction exposure, while the easiest to cover and understand, is the most difficult to define. Debate continues as to whether the exposure arises, or potentially so, when the price list is fixed, or when a firm order is received, or sometime in between when the company has a firm anticipation of a sale.

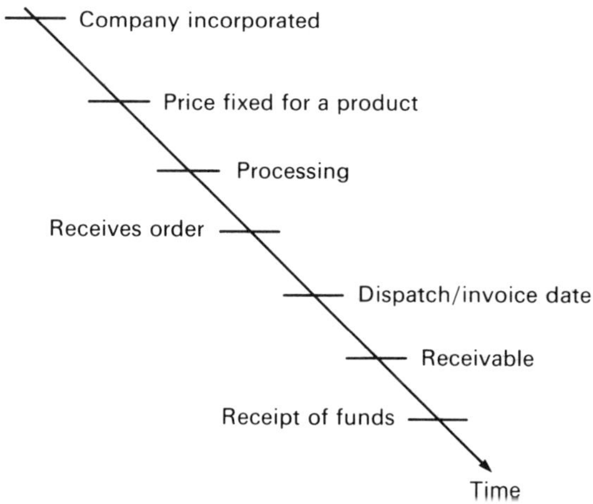

Note: Transaction exposure relates not only to buying and selling raw materials and goods, but also to interest items in currency, royalties or other fees, etc.

Fig. 2.3 Transaction exposure.

Timing risk
This arises when receipts and payments are mismatched as to timing and amount in base or foreign currencies.

Business or operational risk
This is often considered to be within the realm of the strategic planning function. However, it should be mentioned because while changes in the business environment may take time to be quantified financially, steps can be taken in advance by the cash management department to ensure that such contemplated changes can be catered for.

For example, a company has been discounting its receivables, and they have been denominated in its base currency. Due to changes in market practice (led by the dominant player in the market), invoices will be in the overseas currency. The effect is to receive foreign currency instead of base currency. The cash management function needs to ensure it can still discount foreign denominated receivables, and at what costs. If necessary, alternative arrangements will have to be made or new discount facilities set up with other banks.

Country risk
Again, this may be regarded as a strategic planning item, but where a company has dealings with countries which can be described as high risk, certain financial precautions need to be taken. These would be to ensure

payment for goods and services supplied, or a means of dividending funds if the company has subsidiaries in such countries. In instances where this is not possible, companies may be able to enter barter and countertrade arrangements, either with the local government or with other companies in a similar situation.

Bank risk

This is a growing problem for corporates. In general corporates will not mind from whom they borrow, but certainly should mind with whom they deposit. As corporate profitability rises and larger cash surpluses are held, many depositor insurance schemes, such as the Federal Deposit Insurance Corporation (FDIC) in the United States, are insufficient if the bank should fail. In many instances the sums insured are targeted at the individual rather than the corporate depositor.

How are the risks to be managed?

There are four basic approaches that can be taken:

1. Do nothing
2. Hedge everything.
3. Selectively reduce risk.
4. Position taking.

These approaches can apply to each of the risks identified above, ranging from ignoring them to actively second-guessing what might happen.

'Do nothing'

This could be chosen on the basis that the company is best at making its widgets and should continue to make them. The company has no influence on the interest or exchange markets, and in a sense ignores their effect because it feels incapable of predicting their future direction.

'Hedge everything'

It is not possible for a company to hedge all its risks financially, because in attempting to do so it would be creating still more risks. This policy normally refers to those instances where an exposure is readily identified, such as known receipts and payments. The decision basis would be that once these are known they should be hedged irrespective of market conditions.

'Selectively reduce risks'

This is the active management of a risk portfolio: selecting risks, weighting each as to probability of effect, and acting accordingly. This may entail partially hedging exposures to the extent of their probability factor. Unless commercial changes dictate, once a hedge has been set up it is unlikely to be unwound.

'Position taking'

This is an extension of active management, where hedges may be unwound due to financial changes. An alternative is where a company has fundamentally hedged its exposures but decides separately to go 'long' or 'short' of a position in addition. This is distinct from exposure management, and should be controlled and monitored as such.

The culture of the company will dictate which of the four options it will choose in monitoring its exposures. It is a summary of its attitude to risk.

Having considered the broad outlines, the company may clearly set out the parameters within which the cash management department must operate, as in the following example:

1. Analyse, monitor and manage cash flow of funds at group and subsidiary levels:
   (a) Borrow required funds at least cost to the group, within agreed bank facilities.
   (b) Invest surplus funds under security, yield and timing criteria as agreed.
2. Analyse, monitor and manage currency exposure at group and subsidiary levels:
   (a) Buy, or borrow and subsequently buy, currencies to meet requirements.
   (b) Sell, or invest and subsequently sell, currencies received from abroad.
3. Maintain banking systems commensurate with requirements.
4. Manage group's day-to-day relations with bankers, other lenders and potential bankers.
5. In conjunction with other departments and outside advisers, raise long-term finance from lenders or shareholders anywhere in the world.
6. Monitor the observance of a company's financial constraints, whether internally or externally imposed.
7. Advise and guide at group or subsidiary levels on the foreign exchange and interest rate markets.
8. Manage the information system required to ensure the smooth operation of the department and its interface with other departments.

The above list is not an exhaustive one, but merely representative of some of the aspects that should be covered in setting the department's parameters.

Any set 'rules' would be separately identified, such as the following:

1. Borrowed monies on the short-term money market, plus acceptances, should be less than the total committed facilities plus overdrafts. This is to ensure that the company always has a margin in its borrowing capacity, should the short-term market prove inaccessible, and all amounts borrowed have to be repaid.
2. Funds may be placed only with banks and institutions on an approved list, up to the maximum amount designated for that bank or institution. As mentioned earlier, bank risk is of increasing concern. Companies should have an approved list of institutions, based on their own or a rating agency's assessment of the credit risk attached to lending funds to that entity. This list should be approved at board level and updated at least semi-annually.
3. Transactions may be effected only with an approved list of banks or through an approved list of brokers in order to control the number of institutions the company deals with. This can be important during bad times because if a large number of banks are involved in lending to a company, it can create further problems if that company needs to reorganise its debt portfolio. It is important to have a few key relationship banks to which the company can turn when necessary.
4. Funds may be borrowed or deposited, bought or sold using an authorised range of instruments. These would be 'paper' related deposits, such as commercial paper, certificates of deposit or floating rate notes, or options and futures in either the interest or exchange market. The company may wish to limit the use of other instruments until it is sure that any attendant risks are fully understood. This also allows clearance of the tax and accounting implications of their use.

BANKING RELATIONSHIPS

The relationship with banks has already been mentioned in the context of guidelines and rules. Good banking relationships are vital. To achieve these a company must begin by appreciating that a bank is also a company, with shareholders to whom it reports. Thus the bank will be seeking a return on its funds lent while ensuring that the principal will be repayable on its due date. Therefore a company negotiating facilities must allow for compromise, as indeed the bank must, so that neither side is biased. There is always the classic comment of the bank taking away the umbrella when it begins to rain. If banking relationships are good, this should not occur.

In assessing whether or not to lend to a customer, banks will carry out in-depth credit analysis, based on the information available to them. Companies around the world vary in the content and extent of information they are willing to give their bankers, either by tradition or by law. Instances can be cited where bankers are placed in a beneficial position *vis-à-vis* the company's shareholders with regard to the amount of information that is released to them.

The credit assessment will look at the following:

1. The strength and depth of the markets in which the company operates.
2. The company's market shares of its product ranges.
3. The strength of its management, including succession.
4. The company's financial strength over the last three to five years.

If these are not available the bank will project forward likely earnings, growth and product market growth, and will compare all these factors with those of the company's competitors to look at industry trends and where the company stands *vis-à-vis* the industrial sector it is in.

The emphasis on any one or more of these factors will be determined by the type of company being assessed. This will also affect whether security is required before the bank will lend any funds.

There are many types of banking facilities available (see Chapter 7):

1. The overdraft, renegotiated annually as to the amount (and if a small company gradually growing, as to margin too). Prime companies in the UK will pay 1% margin over the bank's base rate. Overdrafts are widely available around the world except in the United States. The overdraft may be secured.
2. The short-term money market line, on an unsecured basis, often called an advised line. This gives the company access to short-term monies, normally up to one year's maturity at short notice, in the money market. A margin would be charged, less than overdraft rates to the borrower, over the bench-mark rate (LIBOR). The margin might vary depending on the bank's own position, so the company is typically quoted an all-in rate to borrow.
3. The acceptance facility, short-term, for the drawing of bills of exchange on the company which can be discounted at the bank. A margin is charged, though usually the quote is given all-in.
4. Committed facilities, where in return for a fee the bank agrees to lend when it is requested to do so. These facilities tend to be of five to seven years' duration, and all terms and conditions are defined in an agreement. Borrowing margins will be stipulated, as will the type of funds that can be borrowed – domestic, Euro or currencies. Events of default will be agreed which will identify when the loans are callable.
5. Various facilities whereby banks will lend against documents of title.

In negotiating facilities a company should always try to maintain as much flexibility as possible in order to cater for changes in circumstances.

CHAPTER 3

Information systems

CHAPTER AIM

To examine the range of information available from internal and external sources; to review methods of receiving information.

Information is vital to the working of any organisation. It must be timely and accurate. This is particularly true in the management of financial situations. The markets are constantly changing in response to new information, all of which must be assimilated and understood in the context of the company's position. If the company is actively managing its financial objectives then action may be required.

Information is supplied to the company or department from internal

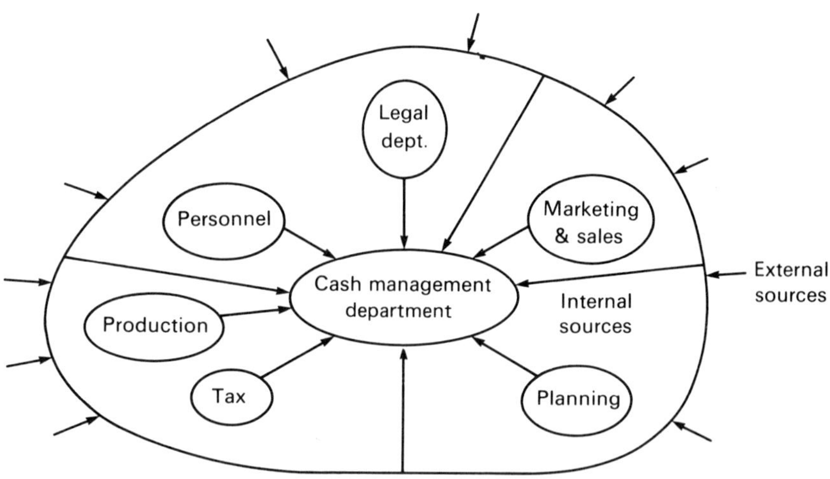

Fig. 3.1 Sources of information.

and external sources (see Fig. 3.1). There is usually a wealth of it available, the difficulty being in sifting through it to identify the key issues.

Information is the base ingredient in forecasting (see Chapter 4). It is also the base ingredient leading to changes in forecasts previously made. Hence any management information system needs to be sufficiently flexible to accommodate this.

INTERNAL SOURCES

The information of use to the cash department will primarily be available through the management accounting reporting system. This will produce, typically, monthly management accounts, quarterly reviews, annual budgets, and annual strategic plans looking forward three or five years or longer depending on the nature of the corporate business.

Strategic plan

On a consolidated basis, the plan will indicate the implied growth of the group. It may include guesstimates of new projects, establishment of new plants or acquisitions, and disposals. While the plan will not indicate details, the inference of the likely requirement for funds and facilities can be made. Where disposals are contemplated, the reverse would be true, requiring the deposit criteria to be revised. The cash manager needs to be aware of these likely developments in order to plan ahead. For instance, if two years ahead a major greenfield site is to be developed abroad, the cash manager should ensure contacts are made early, firstly with bankers of the country in question and secondly with the corporate long-term debt market players, regarding finance. Markets are complex; they should be studied and nuances understood before entering them.

The information contained in the plan will tend to be descriptively biased rather than numbers biased, the object being to assess the business in today's climate and project it forward in the light of anticipated changes. The numbers will reflect this. The numbers produced would be balance sheets and profit and loss accounts over the designated period.

Guidelines may be set down as background to the plan; such assumptions could be interest and exchange rate forecasts, target growth rates, target borrowing rates, etc. In writing the plan each business group will base its figures on the agreed assumptions or will state (and explain) where otherwise. It is important that the common assumptions are broadly followed; otherwise, in assessing resource allocation, like is not being compared with like.

Budget

The budget process is a more detailed annual analysis of each aspect of the business. Like the plan, common assumptions are set within which local management put forward their budgets. Budgets can be set for each 'profit' or 'cost' centre. As a result, a pyramid builds up (Fig. 3.2).

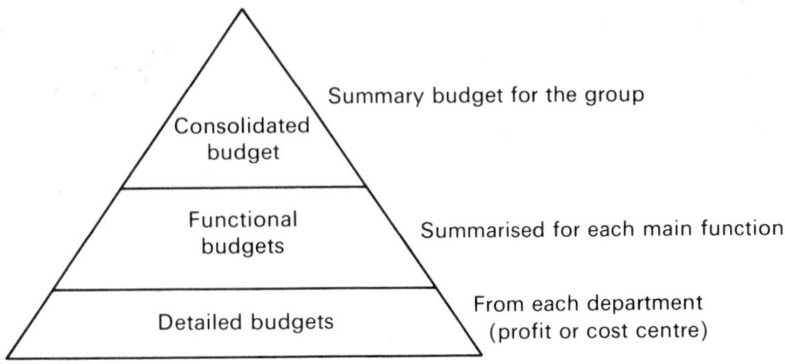

Fig. 3.2 The budget pyramid.

An alternative diagrammatic representation (Fig. 3.3) shows the interaction between the budgets (each box representing a budget).

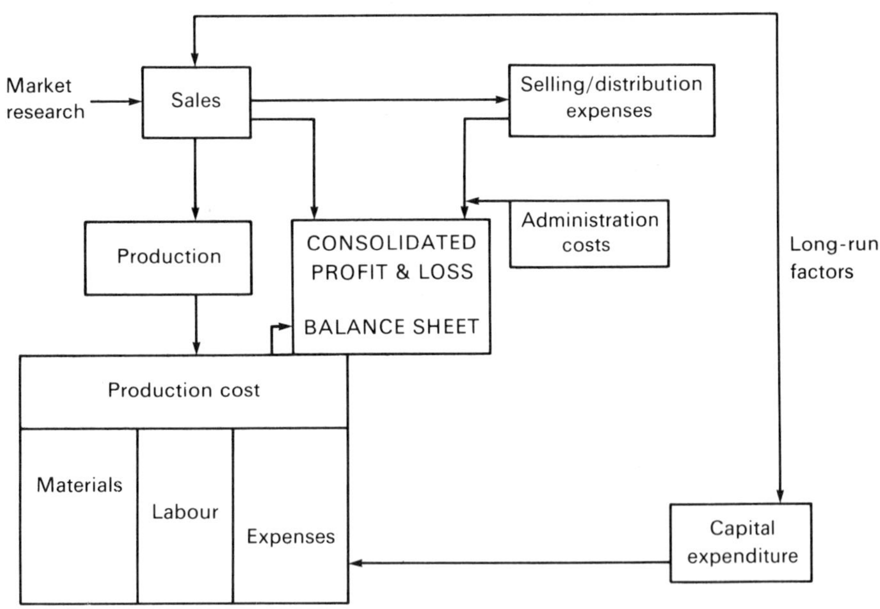

Fig. 3.3 Interaction between budgets.

Because there is interaction between the budgets, they must be collated at a central point. For instance, sales could be forecasting higher turnover, yet production does not have the capacity to meet this.

From the information that the budget process provides, the cash department can estimate likely financing needs for working capital and capital expenditure. The budget will show the phasing over the year, giving indications of, say, quarter-end borrowing levels and cash flow.

Budgets tend to be an annual process, though they may be on a rolling rather than fixed basis. Thus a new month or quarter is added as the previous one is dropped. This has the benefit of always looking forward 12 months, but can be time-consuming and costly to produce.

Traditionally, budgets were not revised during the period to which they refer. However, this view is changing, and budgets tend to be revised as the year unfolds. In other words sales forecasts, costs and profit estimates are changed in the light of economic and operating conditions. The advantage of so doing is that the variance analysis is more realistic, and by inference should lead to improved management control. On the other hand, the variances can be easily explained away.

From the consolidated budgets, special financial budgets will be prepared such as the cash budget and capital expenditure budget. The former is a monthly budget of cash inflows and outflows which are expected to arise from the plans in the consolidated budget. The latter focuses on capital expenditure plans to purchase both replacement and new assets.

Management accounts

These follow the budget process, recording actual performance against budgeted performance. The variances are explained by management in their commentary. Any budget revisions will also be included. The format for the reports might be as illustrated in Fig. 3.4.

The analysis will take the form of monitoring the working capital cycle

	Current month			Cumulative		
Description	Budget	Actual	Variance	Budget	Actual	Variance
Sales						
↓ etc.						

Fig. 3.4 Format for a management accounts report.

ratios (see Chapter 7). The analysis can be shown diagrammatically as a system (Fig. 3.5).

This system serves as a control on the manager so that if working capital levels are rising, these will highlight the problem areas (such as lengthening days inventory and lengthening debtors – the first showing slow-moving stock, due possibly to a downturn in the market or changes in fashion, and the second the possibility of rising bad debts). The cash department is more interested in the remedy than the cause, though understanding the cause may help forecast the time it will take to remedy.

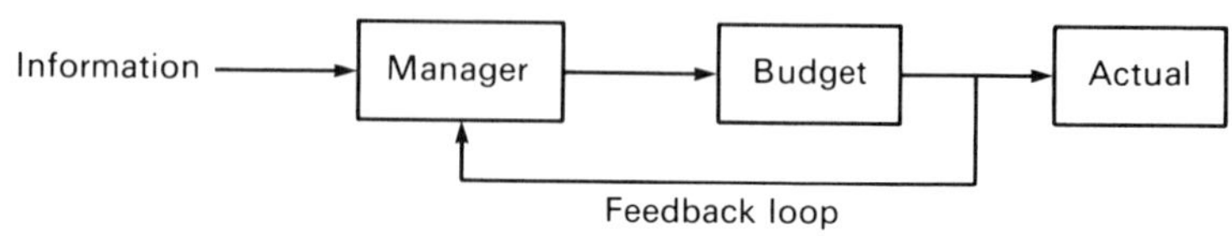

Fig. 3.5 Management accounts analysis system.

Management information systems (MIS)

As with all types of information, management information is of use only if it is accurate and timely. The introduction of information technology can greatly enhance the process. MIS should provide information to support operations, management and decision-making functions within the group.

The value to a cash department is to allow it to play 'what if' scenarios with the raw data in coming to a best estimate forecast for the likely outcome. The data that the department could access would be limited, probably based on a financial modelling package such as a spreadsheet-based one.

MIS is used for cash flow analysis (financial forecasting); balance sheet projections and profit planning; budgeting; strategic planning; and investment and financial analysis. However, the value of MIS is only as reliable as the information fed into it – a fact which is occasionally overlooked.

EXTERNAL SOURCES

There are two types of information from external sources: that pertaining directly to the company, and the general source of information on financial and commercial markets.

The primary source of financial information available externally is from the banks. It is the reporting, daily or otherwise, of the company's account positions. A company should probably be monitoring its cash position daily. As cheques are written and cheques paid in, it is important to ensure timings match so that no unnecessary swings in debit or credit positions are created.

Banks can report differing 'qualities' of information. In the United Kingdom this can be last night's close position or this morning's open position. The difference between the two is the amount held in clearing, which will clear today through the company's account. The only items today's opening position cannot include are any direct debits or credits to the account which will be made through the town clearing or special clearing systems. If nothing is presented, then today's opening will equal tonight's close position. This is important in monitoring the company's cash position (see Chapter 5).

This information can be received in hard copy, as a bank statement, or by telephone or electronically.

The growth of the electronic balance reporting systems over recent years has been widespread. Originally they developed in the United States within the banks, but were released to major corporate clients. Nowadays most banks worldwide either have their own system, or have piggy-backed on another bank system.

Basically they allow access, through a VDU, via a modem, to the bank's own computers or, via a network, to the company's account information (Fig. 3.6).

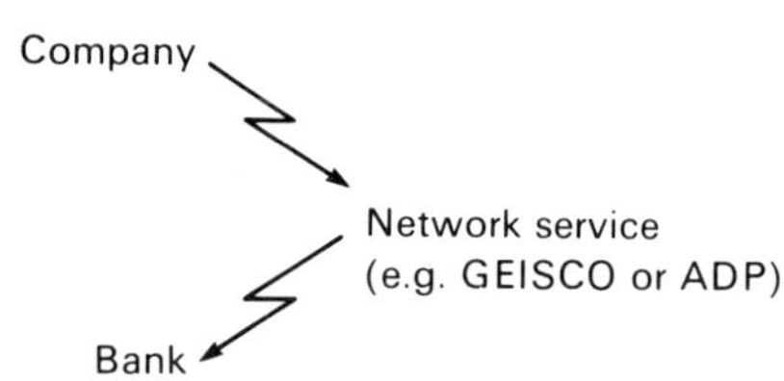

Fig. 3.6 Electronic access to account information

The company will telephone network services, using the password, or will link electronically to the service. Using further passwords it will call up its account information, which can be pulled off on to hard copy at the company's office. Alternatively, the information may be used direct in a spreadsheet format. From this the company will manipulate its balances, adding any other account information from other banks.

It is possible to pick up many banks' balance reports through one telephone call. This occurs when other banks agree to download the particular parcels of information to the network service, to be slotted into the parcel of information of the lead bank. In general, banks are willing to download information; the difficulty arises with the quality of that information. The other banks would naturally favour the company taking their electronic reporting services, and will tend to favour its direct customers in providing a real time information service.

External information regarding the financial markets is widely available, as is comment. The difficulty here is in sorting out what is applicable and what is 'sound'. The range of information sources includes independent forecasters, news agencies, banks, technical forecasters, government bodies, raw data suppliers and so on.

Newspapers

The leading financial daily newspapers around the world provide an excellent basic source of information in their up-to-date coverage of the financial and equity markets. The information is of two sorts: factual reporting of opening and closing prices, the day's range of trading, currency rates, etc.; and some interpretative comment, widely based on discussions held with market participants.

Banks

Nearly all banks have in-house economics departments which will produce for internal and external use fact sheets on countries and currencies, and in-depth analyses. National banks tend to specialise in their own country's economic and currency analysis, but most banks will offer a view on the world's key currencies – the US dollar, the Deutschmark and the yen.

The information is usually provided free, and is available by telex, telefax or hard copy. Some banks produce monthly glossy booklets.

The time horizons reviewed will obviously vary. Most banks give a short-term forecast of up to three months. Some will specialise in producing, say, a quarterly booklet which looks at the longer-term fundamentals underlying the markets.

Some bank economists have better track records than others; some styles will differ. However, they do provide useful background to any given situation.

Specialist forecasters

These may be chartists or technical forecasters, or forecasters who plot the market movement and through momentum analysis predict the future trend of an interest rate or currency rate.

The forecasts by their nature tend to be very short-term, for example, covering 24 hours up to three months. The forecasts will indicate buy, sell and hold positions, and are primarily used by professionals rather than corporates.

Fees are charged for these services, and they are mainly available by telex.

Government bodies

Governments produce a wealth of statistics every month. Some agencies produce synopses of these, for instance central bank booklets.

Statistical information of this sort is valuable in setting the assumptions behind the planning and budgeting processes for key indices such as inflation and growth.

Supra-governmental bodies

Agencies such as the OECD (Organisation for Economic Co-operation and Development), the IMF (International Monetary Fund) and the World Bank are useful sources of further statistical information and analysis. Where a company is commencing operations in a new country, perusal of an IMF or World Bank booklet on that country could prove valuable.

Data suppliers

These companies provide the means through which information can be accessed, e.g. Reuters or Telerate. Both services offer hard copy (teleprint) or a screen and VDU method of accessing information. Both also supply a basic news service, but the bulk of the information is provided by banks and brokers inputting directly to the data banks' real time information on the markets.

This information is real time, though many other systems can provide a database information service which can be accessed, such as Data Resources Inc (DRI) or the Henley Centre in the United Kingdom.

External sources of information regarding the commercial aspects of the markets in which the company is represented are available through trade associations and trade journals. These sources will give good background information for setting the planning assumptions.

CHAPTER 4

Forecasting systems

CHAPTER AIM

To appreciate financial forecasting, based on internal sources of information; to consider assimilation of market information to produce forecasts.

Financial forecasts are produced from the wealth of information available internally (see Chapter 3). These forecasts will vary according to the use to which they will be put. In particular they will vary as to the time horizon they cover, including the number of time periods within that horizon, and as to the format. The format details the items to be forecast and the manner in which that detail is required.

USES OF FORECASTS

In the cash management area, forecasts can be used for a variety of purposes.

Monitoring debt capacity and policy

If the forecast shows levels of borrowing rising significantly, the department will need to ensure that there are sufficient facilities to cover these needs. If there are not, the bankers should be approached for additional lines. If the borrowing levels are higher due to the development of a new product or purchase of new equipment, some analysis of payback will have to be made. Where appropriate, the banker should be informed of the reason why additional funds are required. If the additional funds would put pressure on gearing levels, the bank may seek security.

Used internally, the forecast will highlight subsidiaries' borrowing requirements. This will be used to set the external level of bank overdrafts and, if an internal system operates, the internal level as well. An internal system will mirror the external overdraft unless the borrowing by the subsidiary is intercompany. This will tighten control of the debt levels of the subsidiaries.

Investment strategy and management

The forecast will indicate over what time horizon surplus funds may be utilised. This should be considered in setting an investment strategy. Security is of prime importance, then yield or timing, depending on the company's requirements. If flexibility is important because exact timing is unknown then the company may sacrifice yield, or vice versa.

Currency strategy and management

This is likely to be a shorter-term forecast, for periods of, say, up to six months or one year. In the main the currency forecast will be a consolidated one showing the net position. Further analysis of the individual elements of the forecast may indicate timing differentials, or the extent to which the forecast flows are firm.

Working capital management

This forecast, in its purest form, will be daily, recording the major flows in and out of the company's accounts. The forecast will be combined with the actual bank balances, and a rolling forecast forward can be projected. On such a detailed basis this might only be for one week, but where there is tight cash monitoring against facility levels it may be daily for one month forward. The subsequent periods in the forecast may be weekly or monthly.

As already noted, the format will vary with each forecast. However, each will be a variant of that used in management/financial accounting. A number of ratios are likely to be included to aid analysis (see Chapter 6).

Three examples of format are given below.

1. Accounting format

	Period 1	Period 2	Period 3
Sales			
Cost of sales	______	______	______
Gross profit			
Administration, selling & administration costs	______	______	______

	Period 1	Period 2	Period 3
Operating profit			
Interest charges			
Profit before tax			
Depreciation			
Inflow			
Capital expenditure items			
Working capital			
Tax			
Dividends			
Net increase/(decrease) in borrowings			
Stocks			
Debtors			
Creditors			
Working capital			

Ratios

(a) Profit margin $= \frac{\text{Gross profit}}{\text{Sales}}$

(b) Rate of turnover of working capital $= \frac{\text{Sales}}{\text{Working capital}} = \times$ times p.a.

(c) $\frac{\text{Sales}}{\text{Stocks}}$ or $\frac{\text{Stock}}{\text{Cost of sales}} \times 52$

(d) $\frac{\text{Sales}}{\text{Debtors}}$ or $\frac{\text{Debtors}}{\text{Sales}} \times 52$

2. Cash forecast

	Period 1	Period 2	Period 3
Cash inflows			
Sales			
Cash outflows			
Wages & salaries			
Purchases raw materials			
Services			
Other trading payments			
Net receipts (payments) from trading			
Capital expenditure (purchases/sales)			
Tax			
Dividends			
Net increase/(decrease) in borrowing			

3. Currency forecast
(by currency)

	Period 1	Period 2	Period 3
Currency receipts*			
Currency payables*			
Net currency flow			

* A probability weighting may be requested regarding the likelihood of the flows arising when stated.

This format would be adjusted to take account of any forward contracts.

(by currency)	Period 1	Period 2	Period 3
Currency receipts			
Forward currency purchases			
Net currency flow			

Once these forecasts have been produced it is useful to graph the 'bottom line', to use as a control measure and for quick reference.

ECONOMIC FORECASTS

Drawing up economic forecasts for the group, which can be used as general guidelines for financial forecasting decision-making, is complex.

As seen in Chapter 3 there is an abundance of information. Some companies will rely on professional bodies to produce forecasts for them to their own specifications, while other companies will have an in-house economics department to produce the information. In either case the information may include the following:

1. Product market characteristics.
2. Product market growth.
3. Economic growth factors.
4. Interest rate forecasts.
5. Currency rate forecasts.
6. Inflation estimates.
7. Trade growth.

It is important when looking at such economic forecasts to understand some rudiments of economic theory, such as interaction between the balance of payments, trade flows, invisible earnings and inflation. This is on an international as well as national scale. No company, even if it is a single product wholly domestic-orientated company, is likely to be totally immune to influences of some sort from abroad. A crude example would be where the international markets fear higher inflation in a currency; due to a lack of confidence the currency weakens, and the government's/central bank's response is to raise interest rates. The single product domestic company would be affected by having to pay higher interest charges on its borrowings.

Economic theory is based on supply and demand in determining prices of financial instruments (being akin to commodities) in the market-place. An instrument in its broadest sense can mean an interest rate or currency rate, both being relative to a quantity of money.

There are three categories of market users affecting money markets – commercial users, professional users and governments:

1. Commercial users buy, borrow, sell or invest funds according to the requirements of the businesses they are running. In world monetary flow terms they represent less than 5% of world financial activity, though they have the fundamental need to use the markets.
2. Professional users are those recirculating funds in order to make a 'turn'. As they represent the majority of world financial flows it is their confidence, or lack of it, that will move markets. They have a key role in raising or lowering currency or interest levels because of the sheer volume of funds under their collective control. They have the power to 'test', and break, central bankers' resolve.
3. Governments, through their central banks, will implement monetary policies which will influence the interest in currency rate markets. The reasons for a particular monetary measure might be domestic or based on international co-operation. Their intervention in the markets can cause step changes, but they often find themselves pitted against the professional users, who at the end of the day have more monetary volume to access.

Against this combined weight, commercial users have to forecast, and use the markets.

SCIENCE OR ART?

Over the years there have been attempts to turn forecasting into a science, but it is still very much in the realm of art.

There has been little proof that academic forecasters have consistently been able to outperform the market. In the instances where this has occurred, transferring the 'success' into the real world has proved difficult. In the corporate world there are constraints such as transaction costs, the ability to act immediately, etc. that mitigate against following forecasts rigidly.

There are three broad categories of forecast, as outlined below.

Judgemental

This relies on subjective interpretation of the issues in determining the forecast. It is the 'gut feel' approach to statistics and their implications, government policies, world politics, and the interaction. In order to be consistent, this approach is heavily reliant on the same team of economists putting together the forecast.

Fundamental

These forecasts tend to rely on a few key variables, and are the type most commonly used for planning purposes. Typically the forecaster, using econometric modelling techniques, will extrapolate forward the variables under review, based on key assumptions. These forecasts can easily be sensitised by varying the assumptions to produce differing forecasts. The variables identified would be economic growth rates, interest rates, currency rates and inflation rates. The assumptions could include the price of oil, international levels of trade, political changes and so forth.

The forecasts will of course not be able to cater for events in the markets which lead to step changes in interest and currency rates. Instances of these might be the death of a prominent world leader or a behind-the-scenes agreement between world central bankers.

Technical

These rely on current price movements as the predictor of future movements. Forecasts tend to be for shorter periods, relying on market momentum. They can, however, cope with step changes, as these are built into the current price movements.

In addition to momentum analysis, the technical forecasters look for patterns in the price movements. As a consequence rates will be plotted in a variety of ways to highlight patterns (Figs. 4.1–4.3).

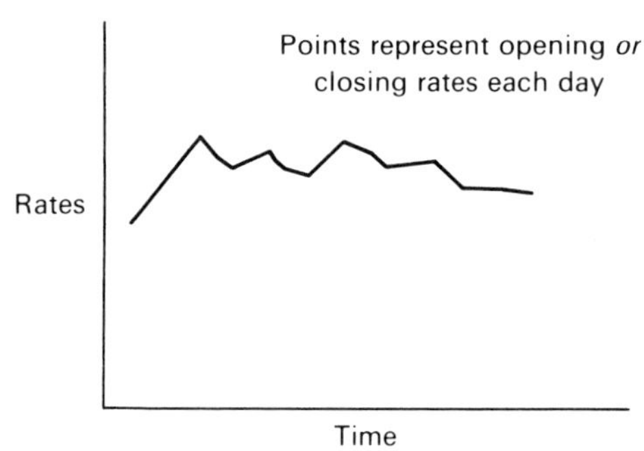

Fig. 4.1 Line chart.

On each chart trend lines will be plotted, itself an art, the skill being to recognise (accurately) the pattern emerging (Fig. 4.4).

A trend line gains significance from its length, or duration, and the

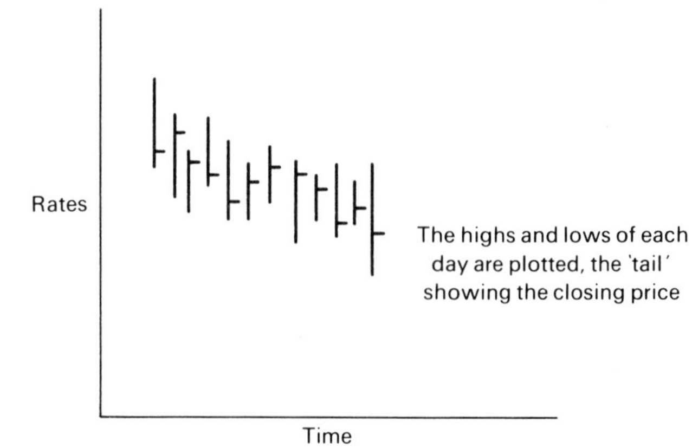

Fig. 4.2 Bar chart.

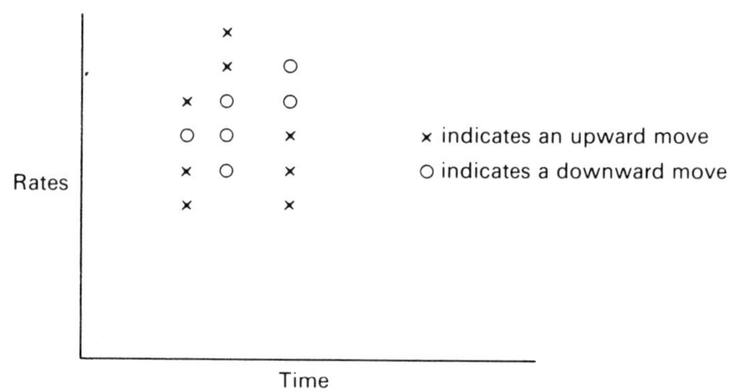

Fig. 4.3 Point and figure chart.

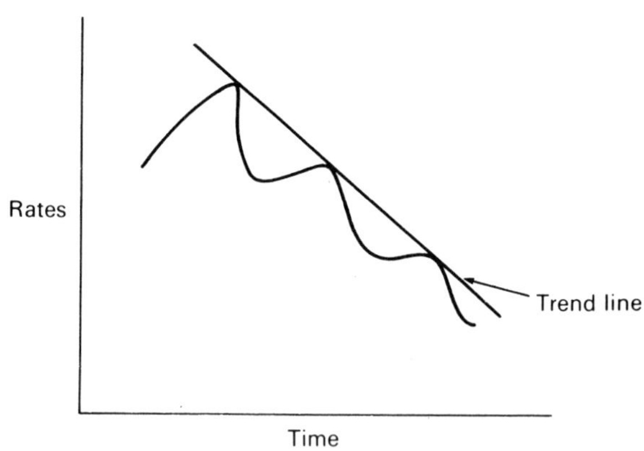

Fig. 4.4 Trend line.

number of times it has been touched or tested. A break in a trend is caused when the penetration of a trend line results in either an actual trend reversal or a slowing down in the pace of the trend (Fig. 4.5).

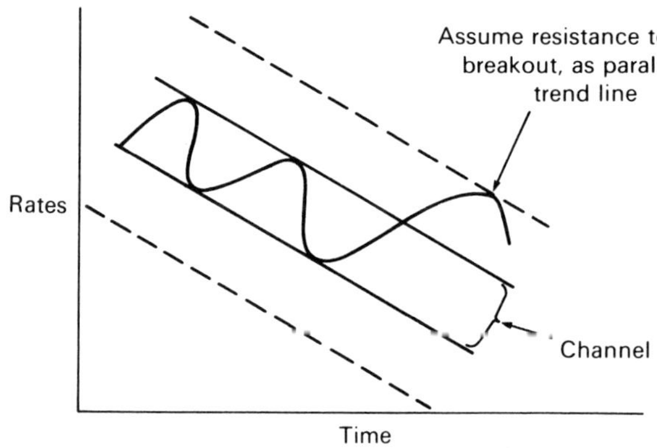

Fig. 4.5 Channel.

The forecast derived from a breakout from the trend is based on the analysis that the currency will move least to the counter-depth before reversing again.

The technical forecasters have produced their own terminology to describe the patterns (Figs. 4.6–4.9).

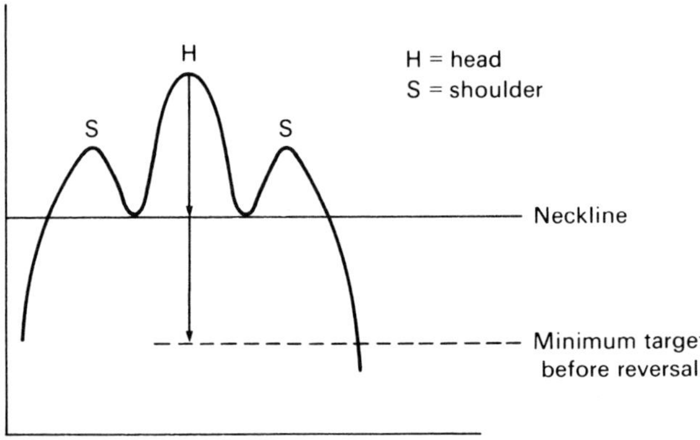

Fig. 4.6 Head and shoulders.

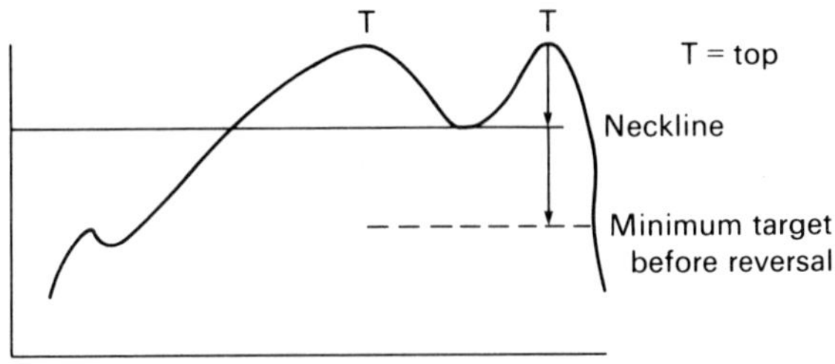

(Double bottom is the reverse.)

Fig. 4.7 Double top.

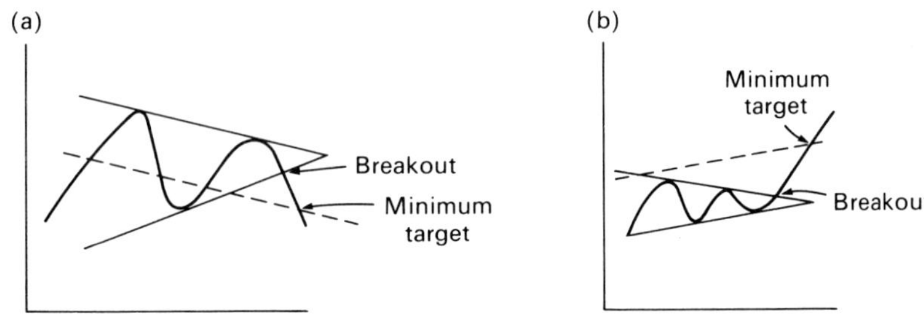

Fig. 4.8 Triangles.

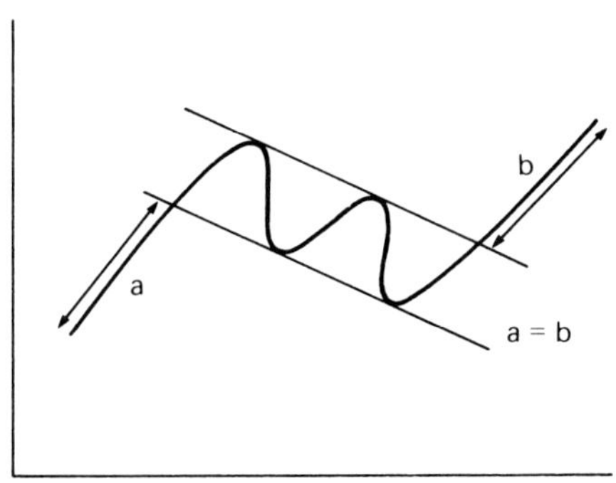

Fig. 4.9 Flag.

CHAPTER 5

Situations management

CHAPTER AIM

To describe how a situation is assessed; to determine how such a situation should be managed.

Exposures will be identified through the internal forecast. Each exposure, or group of exposures, could be called a situation that requires managing. Once identified further analysis should be made:

1. Assessment of the type of exposure, which will affect how the situation might be managed.
2. Quantification of the exposure, and assessment of the 'riskiness' associated.
3. Guidelines set by which the situation will be managed, including action triggers.
4. Priorities set in relation to other situations.
5. Performance monitoring set in place *vis-à-vis* the decision taken.

FURTHER ANALYSIS

Assessment of type of exposure

In looking at the exposure the first assessment is whether it is an interest rate or currency rate exposure, or a combination of the two. Secondly, is it of a short- or long-term nature? In crude terms, since there is always much overlap between currency and interest rates, and between long- and short-term exposures, the split could be represented as follows:

Length of exposure	Currency	Interest rate
Short-term	Transaction	Cash cycle
Long-term	Translation	Balance sheet

Quantification of exposure

This is to assess what the exposure means in real terms today, in the base currency. Once known the position can be 'sensitised'. In doing so a target hedging rate, or hurdle rate, will be set.

For example, ABC is buying machinery abroad. The machine costs DM600,000. The payment profile is 10% with order, 80% on delivery and 10% on commissioning. In the original capital expenditure appraisal a rate of £/DM3.00 was used, against which the payback was 4½ years:

Expected payment profile		
	DM	
Immediate	60,000	
3 months forward	480,000	
6 months forward	60,000	
	600,000	
Today's rates	*£/DM*	
Spot	3.2000	
3 months forward	3.0000	
6 months forward	2.7500	
Quantification		£
60,000–3.20		18,750
480,000–3.00		160,000
60,000–2.75		21,818
		200,568

The quantification at today's rate is £200,568, versus the appraisal figure of £200,000.

This situation can be sensitised by using different exchange rate scenarios. But in the main such exposure, because it is a fixed cost, should be hedged 100% immediately.

Guideline setting

The guidelines set should obviously match the situation to which they refer. They can be set in general for types of exposure, but will need revising for particular instances.

(a) Currency exposure is generally managed in line with the following hedging strategy:

	Assets	Liabilities
Hard currencies (unlikely to devalue)	Increase	Decrease
Soft currencies (likely to devalue)	Decrease	Increase

This applies whether the exposure is of a long- or short-term nature, i.e. whether it is transactional or translational.

(b) Interest rate exposure is managed to maximise yields when investing, though not at the expense of security, and to minimise interest charges when borrowing. This also applies whether the exposure is short- or long-term, i.e. cash cycle or balance sheet.

(c) Hedges should be appropriate in timing to match the underlying exposure. For instance, where a fixed asset is being purchased which has, say, a seven-year anticipated useful life, the borrowing to purchase that item should ideally be for a term of seven years at a fixed rate. In this manner the fixed overhead of running the machine can be truly measured.

This is also true of acquisitions of overseas companies, where the borrowing should be long-term too. In addition, the borrowing should be in local currency in order to reduce translation exposure.

For each given situation which has been assessed and quantified, the target figures at which a hedge should be arranged will have been agreed. As these rates are reached, action is triggered to set the hedge. The method of hedging is a separate decision (see Chapters 6, 7 and 8).

It is important though to set stop-loss targets, in case the original target rate is not reached. These stop-loss positions are also action triggers to set the hedge.

Priority setting

This is the natural follow-on from the previous three sections because the impact of the various situations will have to be explained to senior management and, in conjunction with them, hedging priorities set. Such priorities will vary over time, and in reaction to movements in the financial markets. The short-term exposures will probably be reviewed at least weekly, and certain ones daily. This review will set the specific guidelines such as targets and stop-loss figures. Long-term exposures will probably be reviewed formally every three to six months, and on an *ad hoc* basis in between as acquisitions or capital expenditure proposals arise.

Performance monitoring

This is monitoring the hedge decision itself within the context of the time it was taken. Decisions, particularly major hedges, should always be documented (as a part of the audit trail). It can be useful also to note the general economic background and assumptions used in reaching a decision.

Implied throughout the above is the use of the external forecasts described in Chapter 4 in the general assessment of positions, and of course when quantifying they will be used in the particular.

MANAGEMENT

As an example again, ABC company is a mini-conglomerate with activities in both manufacturing and service industries. It is UK-based, with subsidiaries in Germany and the United States. There is some intercompany trading between the three countries. In the United Kingdom it has two major bankers (clearers). The manufacturing division banks with clearer 1 and the services division with clearer 2. Abroad the subsidiaries use local banks.

Four exposures have been identified in the budget and planning process:

1. The German subsidiary wishes to acquire a local company.
2. The manufacturing division wishes to modernise two of its machines, sourcing the parts from France.
3. The United States will commence supplying Germany on a regular basis.
4. The services division in the United Kingdom is forecasting increased sales and will be cash-generating.

Taking each situation individually, we note the following:

1. This acquisition by Germany will be of a long-term nature. The German-denominated assets of the UK parent company will increase, giving rise to translation exposure at the year-end. In quantifying the amount required, it is DM500,000. In the budget the rate used was 2.95 but it is now 2.75; therefore the cost in sterling terms has increased by £12,327. It is expected that the Deutschmark will appreciate further. The company therefore considers it beneficial to hold Deutschmark-denominated assets. To hedge the translation risk it would normally borrow Deutschmarks, particularly as Deutschmark interest rates are low. However, in view of the relatively small amount of money involved (to the company) and its view that the Deutschmark will continue to appreciate, it decides to purchase the amount required to fund the acquisition. A target is set so that should the Deutschmark begin to depreciate through present levels, the company will borrow Deutschmarks to match the investment. The target exchange rate is £/DM2.75, the rate at which the Deutschmarks were bought to fund the acquisition, with a stop-loss of £/DM2.76. The latter will show a slight loss when the Deutschmarks that had been borrowed are sold for sterling. The later transaction takes place because the company has already made the acquisition by buying

Deutschmarks from sterling; therefore subsequently to borrow Deutschmarks implies it will sell these to replenish the sterling position. In this instance the loss will be one pfennig on DM500,000, or £659.

The performance of this decision will be monitored in the light of actual events. If the Deutschmark continued to appreciate, the decision would have been sensible; if however, the level of DM2.75 was a nadir, then the stop-loss would have been hit.

2. In modernising plant, sourcing from France, the company has two situations to review: currency and interest rates (since funds will be needed to purchase the parts). In quantifying the exposure, the company appreciates it should buy the full amount needed to cover the purchases immediately. This amount is Ffr1,000,000; the current rate being £/Ffr9.6280, this equals £103,864. As the decision policy is to cover immediately, no stop-loss is required. However, the expected life of the upgraded machine is five years, so the company would seek to borrow at a fixed rate for five years. Since the amount is small it is unable to do this cost-efficiently. It therefore decides to borrow on a short-term basis, renewing the borrowing every three months, at which point a new interest rate would be fixed for the subsequent three months. This is not entirely satisfactory because of the variable factor of interest charges within 'fixed' costs. The company therefore decides to set a stop-loss on the interest rate. The current levels are:

1 month	9.25%
2 months	9.25%
3 months	9.25%
6 months	9.50%
9 months	9.75%
12 months	10.00%

This stop-loss is as much a matter of period as of rate. The aim is to lengthen the maturity of borrowing when interest rates have fallen, and the view is that the rates will likely rise rather than fall further. Should this occur during the maturity period, the company would consider a forward transaction, locking in the cost of its borrowing today for value on the future maturity date, say in two months' time. The performance decision measure will again be in response to actual events.

3. The exposures arising on intercompany cross-border trading will be short-term, and will hinge on which party is bearing the transaction exposure. In this instance the United States is invoicing Germany in Deutschmarks, so the former will bear the exposure. In quantifying

the exposure the United States has Deutschmark receivables; it also includes Deutschmark payables. It makes a currency forecast, as follows:

Currency forecast (DM000)	Months					
	1	2	3	4	5	6
Receipts (intercompany)	500	700	500	650	700	500
Payables (third-party)	100	200	1,000	200	50	1,000
Net position	400	500	(500)	450	650	(500)
Cumulative	400	900	400	850	1,500	1,000

In the first instance the company will look at the monthly position, compared with its forecast forward Deutschmark rates. Secondly, it will look at the cumulative position. In essence it would be 'cheaper' for the company to pay Deutschmarks in month 3 from the accumulated receipts in months 1 and 2, and similarly in month 6 from the funds in month 5.

The US$/DM rates are:

Spot	*1.8600*
1 month	1.8550
2 months	1.8500
3 months	1.8400
4 months	1.8450
5 months	1.8375
6 months	1.8325

The company takes the view that it is unsure whether the Deutschmark will appreciate further. There has been much volatility in the market, and market sentiment is that the US dollar will weaken. The company has quantified the Deutschmark input to its product at about 10% of the price. It therefore has a natural hedge of 10%. It decides with this background to manage the net cumulative position rather than the monthly position. Therefore receipts in months 1 and 2 will be placed on deposit when they arrive, to mature in month 3 – similarly DM500,000 of the receipt of DM650,000 in month 5; this will be put on a one-month deposit to meet the payment due in month 6.

The long Deutschmark position that the company has to sell is as follows:

(DM000)		Months			
1	2	3	4	5	6
—	—	400	450	150	—

It decides to sell forward these amounts. If the amounts were larger it might have sold in percentage stages, at target rates with stop rates to cover unforeseen currency movements. To act in this manner would allow the company to take advantage of further Deutschmark appreciation. This would be assessed in the performance monitoring.

4. The services division forecast shows monthly cash generation as follows:

Cash forecast (£000)	Months					
	1	2	3	4	5	6
Sales	650	750	1,000	1,000	1,500	1,500
Raw materials	(400)	(400)	(450)	(500)	(500)	(500)
Expenses	(200)	(200)	(200)	(200)	(200)	(200)
Net	50	150	350	300	800	800
Cumulative	50	200	550	850	1,650	2,450

Initially the exposure to short-term rates is small but it increases rapidly. The company has to look carefully at the yield curve to quantify its exposure. At present the curve is flat but rates are expected to ease in the long term. The division would therefore seek to deposit on a term basis. The feasibility of this depends on how soon the funds may be required, and how frequently funds are received and in what volume. This would be seen on a daily cash flow. The guidelines would seek to cover all these factors. In the instance where rates are forecast to fall, it may be beneficial for the company to borrow immediately for a shorter period and put the funds on deposit for longer periods. Money received in the future will repay the borrowings.

For instance:

	Borrow	Deposit
Rates now		
month 1	10.00	9.875
month 2	9.75	9.675
month 3	9.50	9.375
month 4	9.50	9.375
month 5	9.50	9.375
month 6	9.50	9.375
Rates expected 1 month out		
month 1	9.00	8.875
month 2	8.75	8.675
month 3	8.50	8.375
month 4	8.50	8.375
month 5	8.50	8.375
month 6	8.50	8.375

In this instance the company might borrow £150,000 initially at 10% for one month at a cost of £1,233. The borrowed amount would be added to the surplus of £50,000 at the end of month 1 and the total £200,000 put on deposit for six months at 9.375, earning £9,247. This would compare with £50,000 being deposited for six months at 9.375 plus £150,000 deposited for five months at 8.375 (one month out), totalling £7,474. The principle can be extended.

The performance monitoring would be exact if interest rates did not fall and the latter policy been followed, and there would be a considerable cost to the company.

CHAPTER 6

Managing cash cycle exposure

CHAPTER AIM

To understand the meaning of cash cycle and working capital; to understand techniques available for efficient flow of funds in reducing exposures due to timing differences.

Cash cycle exposure arises as a result of the timing difference between the purchase of raw materials and their ultimate sale after processing (Fig. 6.1). In some industries this can actually be negative, e.g. in a supermarket business, where goods are purchased for resale without any further processing. It is likely that these goods will be sold and cash received prior to the company paying for them. However, the more normal situation is that of a timing gap, which is funded by the company's short-term resources.

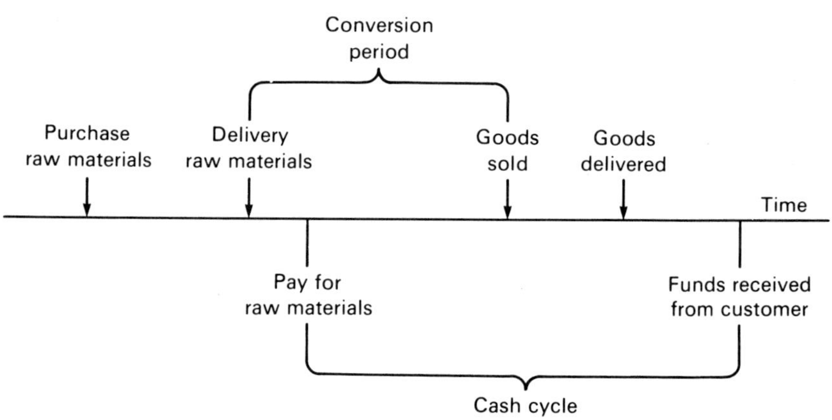

Fig. 6.1 Cash cycle exposure.

WORKING CAPITAL

The short-term resources used to fund the cash cycle are commonly known as working capital – that portion of finance available to a company which is being used to fund its normal operating cycle.

Working capital comprises cash balances; stocks (raw materials, work in progress, finished goods); and debtor balances, generally outstanding receivables from customers less any credit balances – in short, current assets less current liabilities.

To measure working capital, two ratios are commonly used:

1. $\text{The current ratio} = \dfrac{\text{Current assets}}{\text{Current liabilities}}$

2. $\text{The quick ratio} = \dfrac{\text{Current assets less stocks}}{\text{Current liabilities}}$

As a measure of a company's liquidity position these ratios are of limited significance. To have any value they should be compared with the ratios of similar businesses and over time.

A more general ratio which can be used as an intracompany measure is the following:

$$\frac{\text{Working capital}}{\text{Total or fixed assets}}$$

If the company has a high proportion of working capital to total or fixed assets, it is seen as being more resilient. In this context it can be flexible in the use of its resources. However, this will again depend on the type of company. While a large heavy manufacturing company with continuous flow production and high levels of fixed assets may have a high working capital level, it will not be able to react as flexibly to reinvesting its resources as will a wholesale company selling, say, washing machines.

Alternative ratios link the elements of working capital with other parts of the business:

$$\left.\begin{array}{ll} 1. & \dfrac{\text{Debtors}}{\text{Sales}} \\[2ex] 2. & \dfrac{\text{Stocks}}{\text{Sales}} \\[2ex] 3. & \dfrac{\text{Creditors}}{\text{Sales}} \end{array}\right\} \quad \frac{\text{Net working capital}}{\text{Sales}}$$

These ratios are studied in terms of their trends over time rather than in absolute, because they reflect only the situation at a given point. In analysing a trend the company can pinpoint areas of concern, particularly where stock and debtor turnover are translated into days sales in inventory and days sales outstanding, respectively.

1. Days sales in inventory:
   (a) Stock turnover $= \dfrac{\text{Cost of sales}}{\text{Stock}}$
   (b) Days sales in inventory $= \dfrac{\text{Number of days in year}}{\text{Stock turnover}}$
2. Days sales outstanding:
   (a) Debtor turnover $= \dfrac{\text{Sales}}{\text{Debtors}}$
   (b) Days sales outstanding $= \dfrac{\text{Number of days in year}}{\text{Debtor turnover}}$

THE CASH CYCLE

The basic ratios that are used in monitoring the cash cycle have been explained above. Once identified, steps can be taken to reduce the exposures. For example:

ABC Company		Average value per day	
Sales	550,000		1,507
Cost of sales (inc. raw materials 200,000)	350,000	(548)	959
	200,000		
Stocks			
Raw materials	95,000		
Work in progress	50,000		
Finished goods	45,000		
Debtors	100,000		
Creditors	(75,000)		
Average working capital	185,000		

To calculate the total cash cycle in days:

			Days
Raw materials	$= \dfrac{\text{Raw material stock}}{\text{Daily purchases}}$	$\dfrac{95{,}000}{548} =$	173
Less credit	$= \dfrac{\text{Creditors}}{\text{Daily purchases}}$	$\dfrac{75{,}000}{548} =$	(137)
			36
Conversion period	$= \dfrac{\text{Work in progress}}{\text{Daily cost of sales}}$	$\dfrac{50{,}000}{959} =$	52
Finished goods	$= \dfrac{\text{Finished goods}}{\text{Daily cost of sales}}$	$\dfrac{45{,}000}{959} =$	47
Customer credit	$= \dfrac{\text{Debtors}}{\text{Daily sales}}$	$\dfrac{100{,}000}{1{,}507} =$	66
Total			201

This analysis shows that there is a time lag of 201 days in the cash cycle, which essentially has to be funded. It also highlights areas that could be improved, such as reducing the customer credit period from 66 days. It must be appreciated that this is a simplified form of analysis. Companies may be able to break out product lines analysis in this manner, but in general the operation will be looked at in total. Therefore while an overall day cycle can be calculated, in reality funds will continually be received and paid, which will imply the cash flow forecast.

Management

Once the cash cycle has been identified and quantified, it may need to be improved. There are a number of ways that this can be achieved. The responsibilities of physical improvement will lie with the production and sales management; the financial improvement and implications will involve the cash management function.

Stock levels

Any changes introduced by management to alter either the absolute levels of stock held, or the manner in which it is reordered, will have a direct impact on working capital levels. If theories of economic order quantity are applied, it is likely that working capital levels will reduce in the first instance, until the economic level is reached. The reverse may apply to just-in-time methods of supplying customers with finished goods, as the company is required to hold the finished goods stock and supply only when requested by the customer. This will improve the customer's working capital ratios to the detriment of the supplier, unless a compromise can be negotiated.

Debtor levels

Debtor levels, and in particular overdue debts, need constant monitoring.

The first stage is to establish a credit control function to assess the creditworthiness of a customer, process orders, keep the sales ledger, process invoices and collect debts. In a large company this function will tend to be separate from cash management, but in a small company this is not always so. Credit control will be responsible for bad debt collection, ensuring that all cost-effective methods of collecting funds due are used.

The second stage is financial management to reduce debtors. This includes the following:

1. Giving shorter credit periods, which might meet with some customer resistance. In order to retain the level of sales, prices may need to be reduced temporarily. The benefit of reducing credit time can be readily calculated as:

$$\frac{\text{Reduction of debtors Outstanding (days)}}{365} \times \text{sales} \times \frac{\text{average cost of capital}}{100}$$

   This must be weighed up against any loss in sales due to the 'aggressive' move of cutting credit periods. Again, the impact will vary from company to company and product to product, in line with the supply and demand profile of the product in question.
2. Giving discounts for prompt settlement will encourage late payers to pay earlier, but those who already pay promptly will get the benefit of the discount. The decision therefore becomes a matter of discretion. If the proportion of late payers to prompt payers is high then it may be worth considering. If the situation is reversed it probably will not be since in order to be attractive the discount may need to be more expensive than the cost of carrying the debt initially. If the company is seeking an improvement in cash flow and gearing, then this will be sustainable.

To assess the effectiveness of a discount policy, the before and after must be compared. For example, ABC Limited has monthly sales of 100,000. Customers' payment profile is typically 50% in month 1, 25% in month 2 and 25% in month 3. It is decided to offer a 2% discount for payment within month 1. Experience showed that the improvement came from those who had previously paid in month 2. The current cost of finance is 12% per annum.

	Month		
	1	2	3
Old system	50,000	25,000	25,000
New system	70,000	5,000	25,000
Discount (Cost) 2% × 70,000	1,400		
Interest saved:			
$\frac{12}{100} \times \frac{1}{12} \times (70{,}000 - 50{,}000) = 200$			

If the outcome had been different and the improvement had been in the late payers, the situation would have been as follows:

	Month		
	1	2	3
Old system	50,000	25,000	25,000
New system	90,000	5,000	5,000
Discount (Cost) 2% × 90,000	1,800		
Interest saved:			
$\frac{12}{100} \times \frac{1}{12} \times 20{,}000$	= 200		
+ $\frac{12}{100} \times \frac{2}{12} \times 20{,}000$	= 400		
Total interest saved	600		

Therefore in both instances the discount should not be given because the total costs outweigh the benefits in monetary terms.

However, if the old system had shown late payers initially then the discount would be break-even:

	Month		
	1	2	3
Old system	—	—	100,000
New system	100,000		
Discount (Cost) 2% × 100,000	2,000		
Interest saved:			
$\frac{12}{100} \times \frac{2}{12} \times 100{,}000$	= 2,000		

In financial terms the calculation is break-even, but the cash flow position would have been enhanced, particularly if it is viewed that interest rates will shortly rise.

In the latter example the discount offered would have to be less than 2%, e.g. a rate of 1.5%. In order for the discount offered and taken up to be beneficial to ABC Limited:

Discount 1.5% × 100,000 = 1,500	
Interest saved:	
$\frac{12}{100} \times \frac{2}{12} \times 100{,}000$	= 2,000

3. Trade only for cash, which while ideal is not wholly practicable, and indeed would tend to lose customers.
4. Factor receivables by selling them at a discount in order to receive

funds now. The factor is then responsible for collecting debts. This system, like discounting to the customer, can be costly since the cost of the discount is typically higher than the carrying cost of an overdraft. It is often seen as a mechanism to stave off financial crisis. However, there are various forms of factoring, so the customer would not necessarily be aware that receivables were being factored.

Creditor levels

A company will try to stretch its creditors in order to give itself extra cash flow liquidity. However, by becoming known as a late payer the company can do itself a disservice. Any company that is consistently late will probably be paying more for its goods, as suppliers will factor in the late payment costs. The service from the supplier may deteriorate. Supplies of goods may be cut off. Ultimately the company's credit rating might be affected, which would lead to other difficulties. When a company is offered discount terms for earlier payment, these need to be assessed on two accounts. The first is whether the annual discount rate compensates for the opportunity cost of early payment. The second is consideration of the extra cost in processing individual invoices separately in order to take advantage of the discount.

For example, ABC Limited normally pays its suppliers in the third month after invoicing. It is now offered a 3% discount for payment within one month on invoicing. Payments are 12,000 per month, and the current cost of finance is 12% per annum:

1. In order to pay two months earlier than intended ABC will have to fund 24,000 @ 12% per annum, the cost being 2,880 on a per annum basis.
2. Each month ABC will gain a cash discount of 3% × 12,000 = 360 × 12 = 4,320 per annum.
3. The gain to ABC in accepting the discount, on a per annum basis, is 4,320 − 2,880 = 1,440.
4. From this sum of 1,440 should be deducted any additional administration costs.

MANAGING THE EXPOSURE

Once a set of optimum targets for the ratios has been achieved by taking into account commercial reasons, and smoothing the element of working capital, the residue can be identified as a cash cycle exposure. This exposure needs to be managed, as it will be at risk to movement in interest rates and perhaps currency rates (see Chapters 4 and 5).

First stage

The first stage of management is the practical one of ensuring the timely receipt of payment for goods.

Receipts

Efficient cash management implies that funds received are cleared into the company's account as soon as possible. The mechanisms set up thus need to ensure this:

1. If a company is receiving sterling amounts there must be an account in sterling into which funds can be paid.
2. If the company frequently receives cheques in excess of £10,000, special clearance procedures should be set up:
   (a) A City account is set up at a branch of one of the clearing banks within the City designation. This is noted by the presence of a 'T' after the sort code on the face of the cheque (see Appendix: Banking systems – United Kingdom). If the customer has a 'T' on their cheques, this will indicate a town clearing cheque; and if presented to that bank, same-day funds are obtainable. If convenient, in these instances it is worth having cheques delivered to the bank for subsequent presentation.
   (b) If the company is located outside the City of London, requests for special clearance can be made for large items, or items where the creditworthiness is in doubt. This process can be same-day but is more usually 'following day' clearance.

   Other sums would be paid into the account in the normal way, cleared (through the country clearing system, i.e. not the town system), and assigned value of one or two days.
3. A company can receive funds direct into its accounts via telegraphic transfers from a third party or by direct credit. The difference between the two is that the latter tends to be on a regular basis. Both, however, will give access to cleared funds. This is the most efficient way to receive foreign currency funds.
4. Where a company receives foreign currency in the form of cheques, quick clearance systems are important. Cheques drawn on foreign banks abroad have to be returned there for clearance. Therefore, where high-volume cheques are being sent to the company denominated in a foreign currency, all drawn on one bank, the company should open a current account at a local branch of that bank. This will speed up the clearance time significantly. If there is no local branch, then the company should choose a bank that has a reciprocal arrangement (correspondent bank) with the foreign bank. The lines of communica-

tion between the two banks should be such that clearance will be quicker. If not, the account should be moved to another bank.

5. Where a company receives money in the form of a bill of exchange or promissory note, it has the option of discounting it in the market to receive available funds. The decision as to whether this should be done will rest on the acceptability of the company's name on whom the bill is drawn, i.e. its creditworthiness, combined with the cost of discounting. If the bill is discounted through the company's own bank, the funds will be paid into the account directly. There is a risk exposure if the bank will only accept the bill with recourse. This implies that if the customer does not pay the face amount of the bill on the due date, the bank is entitled to claim the funds from the company.

The system of same-day value funds is widespread around the world, in line with local banking practices. For instance, in the United States funds can be made available through the Fed funds system. Alternatively, cheque clearance times can be speeded up by using the lockbox service. Cheques are mailed by customers to the lockbox address rather than to the company's own address. At the lockbox (held at a bank) the cheques are processed and the funds credited to the customer's account by the next day. Any cheques paid in locally by the customer can be credited to the main account, again one day later, by a direct credit transfer between the local and lockbox banks. Lockbox locations are chosen with reference to the mail times between locations in order to cut down mail float time. From all sources, therefore, funds are speedily paid into a concentration account, from which they may be dispersed or invested (see Appendix Banking systems – United States).

Payments

If a company has an efficient method of paying its suppliers, it can 'afford' to pay on the final due date. If its systems are not efficient, the company may have its creditworthiness questioned. Payment methods include the following:

1. Payments by cheques can be on the town clearing or country clearing basis; the choice will affect the timing assigned to that cheque for anticipated clearing. Some companies may deliberately introduce delay by using obscure banks at distant locations. In the United States this is known as remote disbursement. It is generally frowned upon and may give the company a bad name. It is not so common in the United Kingdom because of the size of the country and quicker postal services, leading to a more efficient clearing system.
2. Standing orders on an account are instructions by the customer to the

bank to pay regular sums to a particular recipient. These instructions cannot be altered save by the customer.

3. Direct debits on an account are instructions from a customer authorising the bank to debit the account in line with the instructions received from the recipient of the funds. In general direct debits should not be entered into except where the system allows the company to query the debit in advance of its being effected. This system has been introduced through BACS (Bankers' Automated Clearing Services), which allows for the direct settlement of trade invoices. The amounts due for settlement are pre-agreed between customer and supplier; the supplier then makes up a tape or delivers it to the bank. This tape is played through BACS, which automatically debits the customer's account and credits the supplier's account. The day that this tape is run normally takes into account the clearing time forgone by the customer no longer sending cheques.
4. Currency payments can be made by cheque, by telegraphic transfer through the bank (where they exchange the currency), or by direct transfer or electronic means debiting the company's own currency account. Payments in currency other than by cheque are for value two business days hence as it takes this length of time for telexes to be exchanged between banks, so that on the second business day funds will clear from one bank's account to the other. On that day the customer's currency account would be debited, though the recipient may not receive the funds that day. In normal circumstances this should occur, but in some countries local banking practice dictates otherwise.
5. Electronic payments are a means to speed up the payment process and reduce the paperwork involved in effecting a transfer of funds. Inherent in releasing funds electronically is a password system upon which the bank can act. If this security system has been breached within the company, it is to the customer's account. Electronic payments may be of two types:
   (a) Prespecified, where the basic data regarding the transfer are held within the system. All that is input is the amount, value date and any required reference.
   (b) Free format, where the details of the payment are put in from scratch.

   The former is more secure than the latter though, compared to a telephone call, confirmed subsequently in writing, it could be said that the second method is just as secure (see Chapter 9).
6. Payments can be made by way of bills of exchange or promissory notes. This gives the supplier the option of discounting the bills in the

market to receive funds in advance of the due date. As long as the company has no concern in having its paper in the market, it is an efficient means of settlement. The concerns might be, firstly, that it will be seen what credit terms the company is trading on, for instance three-month bills. Secondly, it may affect the credit rating of the company in that most account settlements are on open account, i.e. payable when due, not against paper promises to pay, i.e. bills of exchange.

Second stage

The second stage of management is similarly practical, but pertains to the financing of the cycle.

The external methods of financing both interest rate and currency rate cycle exposures are detailed in Chapters 7 and 8 respectively. Below are outlined some of the internal techniques that a company might use in managing the cycle exposure.

Leading and lagging

Leading and lagging is the process of adjusting the timing of payments and receipts to take advantage of anticipated interest or exchange rate movements. It may be done intragroup or relative to third parties.

For example, ABC company has a series of large payments to make on a contract over a period of six months. It anticipates that interest rates are going to rise. It therefore would like to take advantage of lower rates now and lock in its borrowing cost (Fig. 6.2).

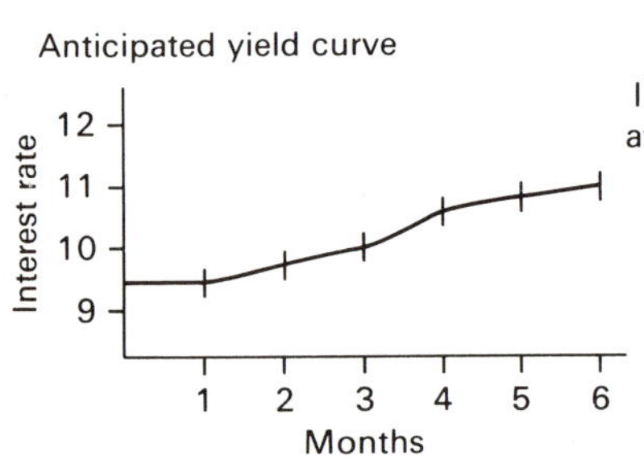

Interest rates at end month	
1	9.50
2	9.75
3	10.00
4	10.50
5	10.875
6	11.00

Payment profile at end month	
1	1,000,000
2	–
3	500,000
4	500,000
5	2,000,000
6	250,000

Fig. 6.2 Leading and lagging.

If the interest rate out-turn is as predicted, the cost to the company would be:

End of month	Outstanding	Rate	Interest cost (ignoring interest on interest)
1	1,000,000	9.50	7,808
2	1,000,000	9.75	8,014
3	1,500,000	10.00	12,329
4	2,000,000	10.50	17,260
5	4,000,000	10.875	35,753
6	4,250,000	11.00	38,425
		Total	119,589

If the whole amount of 4,250,000 were borrowed and paid in month 1, the interest cost over six months would be 230,547, with a total owing of 4,480,547. However, in offering to pay the whole amount up front the company would expect to receive a discount. If this amounted to, say,

$$2.8139\% \quad \left(\text{or } \frac{119{,}589 \times 100}{4{,}250{,}000}\right),$$ interest at 9.5% on the reduced principal

payable would equal 193,507, making a total payable of 4,323,918. This would be an overall saving of 156,629 or 3.68% of the principal sum.

Had the situation been reversed and the company expected rates to decline, then it would try to negotiate the weighting of payments at the end of the period.

In negotiating flexible payment terms, the company has to be mindful of commercial considerations: what is beneficial to one party can be detrimental to the other. Of the two instances cited, the first would actually benefit both parties, with reduced cost to ABC company and improved cash flow for the supplier. In the second instance ABC company would benefit from late payment, but the supplier would be strained in carrying the cost of finance from the original profile. Stage payments in contracts are often introduced as settlement against agreed performance, and it may therefore be difficult to move away from the concept. If this is so then interest rate options, futures or future rate agreements can be entered into to shield the company from rises in interest rates (see Chapter 7).

Leading and lagging is more typically used in the context of cross-border exposures, to take advantage of anticipated revaluations or devaluations of currency rates relative to each other.

For example, ABC company has to pay for raw materials in three months' time. The present £/DM rate is 2.90 and the three-month outright rate is 2.80 (see Chapter 8). The cost of the raw materials is DM550,000:

(a) Purchase DM today @ 2.90 = £189,655
or (b) Purchase DM forward @ 2.80 = £196,428

The preference would be to buy Deutschmarks today, and therefore pay early. As with the interest rate 'leading', a discount may be offered for prompt payment, which would make this option more attractive. However, if the company felt the Deutschmark would weaken against sterling over the three months, it would hold off purchasing and paying out the currency. If the company was very unsure as to the direction of the trend, it could purchase a currency option or futures contract, or range forward (see Chapter 8).

In essence, regarding currency-led leading and lagging, the importer would delay payments in a currency expected to devalue and conversely bring forward payments in a currency expected to revalue. An exporter meanwhile is in the reverse position; it would chase receipts in a weakening currency and delay those in a strengthening currency.

As already noted, there are various commercial considerations in these actions. It is for these reasons that leading and lagging tends to be operated on an intra-group basis, where there is more leeway to take advantage of interest and currency situations. It is important though that where this takes place, the performance criteria of the companies involved are adjusted for the leading and lagging process, in particular any additional interest costs.

For leading and lagging to be successful within a group, it is prudent to have a central management team (cash management) to control and regulate the leads and lags. Secondly, the flow of intercompany transactions should be such, and in those currencies, that would warrant the process.

During the 1960s and 1970s, multinationals used this mechanism to 'shift' profits into tax-favourable areas. As a result some countries, notably in South America, now impose constraints via exchange control requirements which limit these activities.

In summary, the advantages are the fine tuning of the group's liquidity management. It is the first stage in netting and matching flows (see later). It can be a more appropriate form of intercompany financing than intercompany loans due to local regulations, tax rates or withholding taxes on interest flows. The system does however require good control with flexible, efficient payment mechanisms; and because of commercial considerations with third parties, it tends to be used on an intragroup basis.

Price considerations

This is a technique employed with particular reference to currency cycle exposure. The considerations relate to the currency of the invoice, whether in base currency (that of the exporter), local currency (that of the importer) or a third currency (according to market practice). In the last instance market practice can be that dictated by the dominant supplier to the market, or by international forces such that all trades in a commodity type are in that currency.

In setting a pricing policy in currency, reference should be made to the forward market rates and the likely out-turn currency forecast within and external to the company (see Chapters 3 and 4). Pricing is, however, a commercial decision, negotiated between the customer and the company. The role of the cash management department is to advise, to ensure that efficient mechanisms exist for receiving funds and getting good value as soon as practicable, and to monitor the exposure.

If a currency is highly volatile, some companies will use currency protection clauses rather than constantly readjust the price lists. This will allow price adjustment if the currency trades outside a given band; however, this can be difficult to monitor, and cater for, in exposure management.

Matching and netting

These two systems are most effectively run if there is a central cash management function.

Matching

Matching is a process of offsetting payments and receipts in currencies with respect to timing and amount. In practical terms, this can be achieved only by running a network of currency deposits/overdraft accounts. All currency receipts from group transactions are paid into these accounts and all currency payments are made from them. The payments may be lump sums to subsidiary accounts, from which third-party suppliers will be paid, or the central department running the accounts may handle the third-party payments direct. The system will largely depend on the volume of payments, their value, and the efficiency of having sub-currency-holding accounts. A further alternative is to allow the subsidiaries access to debit the main group currency account in making payments. This removes the need for sub-holding accounts, but can give rise to control problems (see Chapter 9).

The benefit of matching is the saving of the bank's spread between the buying and selling rates of the currency versus the base currency (see

Chapter 8). In addition, exposure management is eased since the group is looking at a net amount of currency, and in turn an average rate for that pool of currency.

The latter point touches a difficult management issue – that of managing a 'pool' of currency. There are a number of ways such a central system can operate:

1. All currency transactions are at the 'pool' rate, set on weekly, monthly or budgeted rates, irrespective of actual market rates. In monitoring the profit performance of each subsidiary this arbitrary setting of the pool rate would have to be taken into account.
2. All currency transactions are at the current spot rate, irrespective of whether the currency is being bought from or sold to the centre.
3. All currency transactions can reflect market rates. This will lead to the reintroduction of the banker's spread, but on an intragroup basis rather than externally. The 'spread' could be used to offset central function costs, and so be regarded as an administrative charge.

An extension of matching is the requirement that all currency flows, be they spot or forward, must be transacted through the central function. This allows the subsidiary to hedge itself by buying or selling the currency, leaving the central function the responsibility of managing the overall group exposure. Rates would typically be offered to the subsidiaries on a market basis, i.e. in line with the then current spot and forward rates.

The overall position may or may not be 'laid off' in the market, depending on the central viewpoint regarding currency trends and volatility.

The problem with this system is that there will be few perfect hedges as to amount and timing, so the centre will always be managing a mismatch position, be it on a daily, weekly or monthly basis. Additionally, there will be a mismatch as to the rates for the various transactions. The company selling currencies for the base currency will be seeking to sell them at the opposite time at which a company will be buying currencies. The centre, in the middle, needs an efficient information flow to manage the net position. If this does not exist, or if from time to time the trend of the market so dictates, the centre may well cover one side of the transaction and leave the other unhedged. An example will illustrate this situation.

Exchange rate profile:	6 January £/DM	24 January £/DM
Spot	2.7850	2.8920
1 month outright	2.7700	2.8770
2 month outright	2.7550	2.8620
3 month outright	2.7450	2.8500

All transactions are booked through the centre.

(a) On 6 January Subsid. A decided to sell forward to the centre its receivables of DM100,000 for the next three months.

Month	Subsid. A receives £	Centre receives DM
1	36,101	100,000
2	36,298	100,000
3	36,430	100,000

(b) On 24 January Subsid. B decided to buy forward from the centre its payables of DM150,000 for the next three months.

Month	Subsid. B receives DM	Centre receives £
1	150,000	52,138
2	150,000	52,411
3	150,000	52,632

(c) In the first instance it can be seen that the centre is short of DM50,000 per month. This it can buy in the market at a cost of:

Month	Centre receives DM	Centre pays £
1	50,000	17,379
2	50,000	17,470
3	50,000	17,544

(d) If the centre had taken no action and was willing to match the currency flows in amount and subsequent timing through the use of currency accounts, the result in sterling terms would have been:

Month	Centre Receipts	Centre Payments	Net
1	52,138	(36,101 + 17,379)	(1,342)
2	52,411	(36,298 + 17,470)	(1,357)
3	52,632	(36,430 + 17,544)	(1,342)
			(4,041)

(e) If the centre was of the view on 6 January that the currency would weaken against sterling and if permitted within its departmental parameters (see Chapter 2), it would have sold the Deutschmarks into the market in order to reduce its exposure to loss.

Netting

Netting is a matching system of intergroup cash flows, allowing a reduction in the volume and value of intercompany settlements. Typically, these settlements are in the same currency (Fig. 6.3), but systems exist for multicurrency netting.

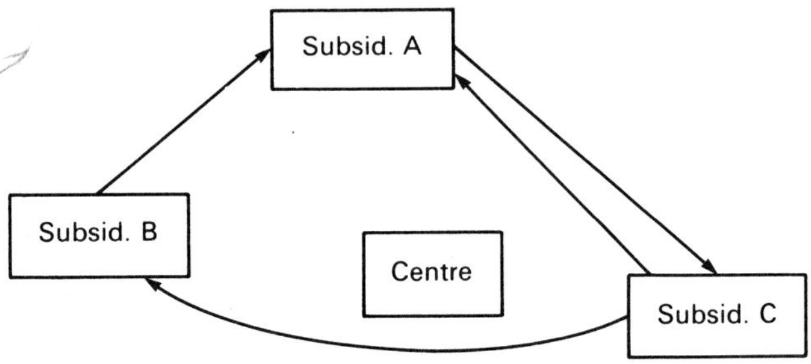

Fig. 6.3 Netting system – same currency.

The flow of funds between Subsids A and C would be netted such that one payment rather than two is made.

		US$
Subsid. A owes Subsid. C		524,000
Subsid. C owes Subsid. A		216,000
	Net	308,000

The net payment would be US$308,000 from Subsid. A to Subsid. C.

For a multicurrency system (Fig. 6.4) to operate effectively the centre would play a key role in the settlement process. It would set the settlement rate at which all flows would be transferred into the respective base currencies, and would ensure payment to each subsidiary in its base currency in order to reduce that subsidiary's exposure to currency fluctuations. The system is designed for companies with a high volume of cross-border intercompany trade. Typically, netting centres have been set up by multinational companies in the Benelux countries, where such centres get beneficial tax treatment.

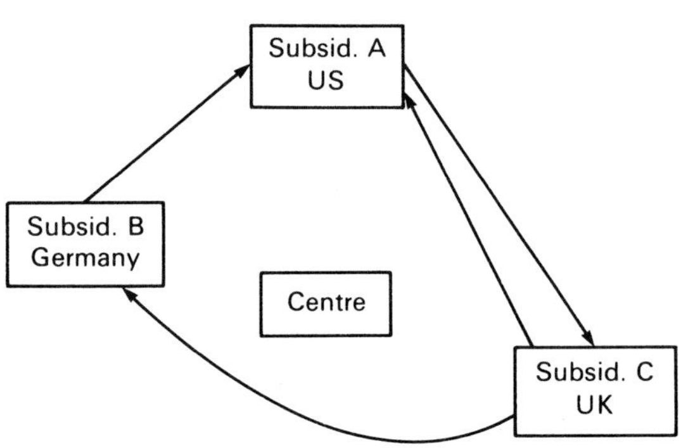

Fig. 6.4 Netting system – multicurrency.

Payments

Subsid. A owes Subsid. C US$524,000
Subsid. B owes Subsid. A DM350,000
Subsid. C owes Subsid. A US$216,000
Subsid. C owes Subsid. B FFr987,000

Settlement day

£/US$	1.5190
US$/DM	1.8160
£/FFr	9.1785
DM/FFr	3.3270

The centre computes the base currency equivalents on the basis that all settlements are through it.

(a) The process is illustrated in Fig. 6.5.

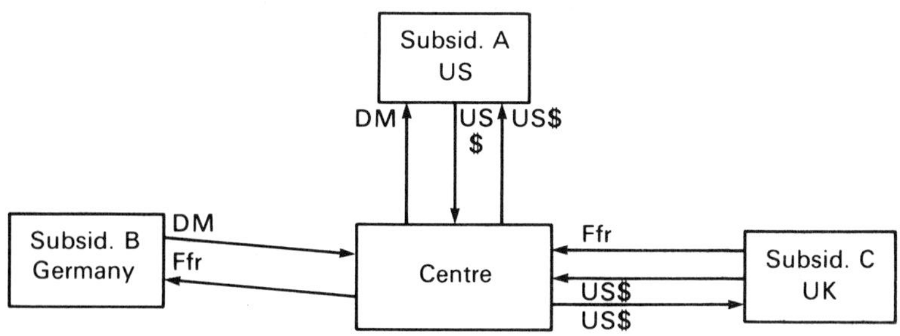

Fig. 6.5 Multicurrency process.

(b) By subsidiary:

(i) As Subsid. A is a US company, it will pay in US$ equivalent and receive in US$ equivalent:

A owes C	= US$(524,000)	
A is owed from B	= US$192,731	(equivalent of DM)
A is owed from	= US$216,000	
A's net position	US$(115,269)	

This would be paid to the centre.

(ii) Subsid. B is a German company and so would receive and pay in Deutschmark equivalents:

B owes A	DM(350,000)	
B is owed by C	DM296,664	(equivalent of FFr)
B's net position	DM(53,336)	

This would be paid to the centre.

(iii) Subsid. C. is a UK company and so would receive and pay in sterling equivalents:

C owes A	£(142,199)	(equivalent of US$)
C owes B	£(107,534)	(equivalent of FFr)
C is owed by A	£344,964	(equivalent of US$)
C's net position	£95,231	

This would be received from the centre.

Figure 6.6 shows the end result in diagrammatic form.

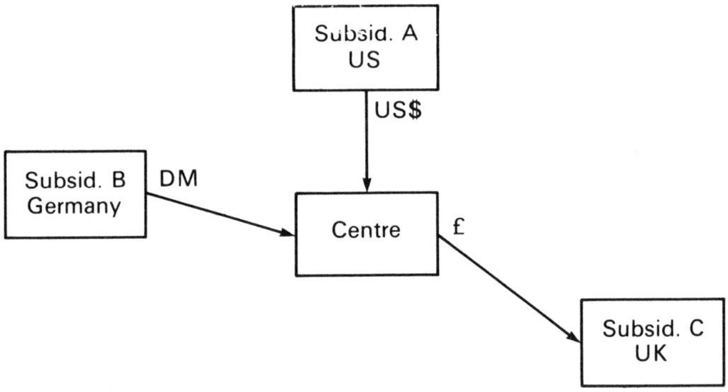

Fig. 6.6 Multicurrency result.

As a consequence, at the end of the day each subsidiary and centre would be all square in that all currencies were exchanged at the same rates. The centre would have a residual exposure as it would have to lay off the currency mismatches with the market, at perhaps differing rates from those used internally.

The final stage from netting centres is to refine the process and set up a reinvoicing centre through which all sales would be routed. The management of the resultant exposure would be similar to the matching and netting systems, though there might be more scope for matching timings and thus rates more accurately.

CHAPTER 7

Managing interest rate exposure

CHAPTER AIM

To understand the terminology and the methodology of the money markets; to understand the use and application of market techniques in managing interest rate exposure.

The extent to which a company has interest rate exposure to manage will depend on the following:

1. The company's attitude to risk.
2. The role finance plays within the performance measurement system of the company.

For instance, a subsidiary of a company is being monitored at the pre-interest level, either on return on capital or on a profit margin basis:

1. $\text{Return on capital} = \dfrac{\text{Profit before tax, interest and dividends \%}}{\text{Total capital employed}}$

2. $\text{Profit margin} = \dfrac{\text{Profit before tax, interest and dividends \%}}{\text{Sales}}$

On these performance criteria there is no immediate incentive for the company regarding tight financial control, or the efficient and effective use of funding. Finance and its costs or benefits cannot be regarded as a 'sunk' item. Indeed, in this day and age, with such volatility in the markets, the interest rate portfolio should be actively managed within guidelines (see Chapter 5).

Interest rate management revolves primarily around the use of banks and the money markets. A few years ago smaller companies tended to look only to their local bank for finance, but this has now changed as foreign banks and other clearing banks have realised the potential lending opportunities to sound smaller companies. As a result, access to the money markets direct, through a range of banks or via brokers, has been greatly improved. Another improvement has been the banks setting up customer liaison desks in their dealing rooms to specifically discuss interest rate or currency problems and market conditions with their customers. This allows the bank's own dealers, while they still ultimately provide quotes to the customer through the liaison desk, to deal predominantly with the interbank market – where time is of the essence and the amounts involved tend to be larger.

The trend has affected not only the money markets but also the foreign exchange markets, and in centres other than London.

SOME DEFINITIONS

Bid

This is the rate at which a bank will buy funds, i.e. quote for deposits. The money market quote can be identified by centre, e.g.:
LIBID – London interbank bid rate;
FIBID – Frankfurt interbank bid rate;
BIBID – Brussels interbank bid rate.

Offer

The rate at which the bank will sell funds, i.e. the borrowing rate. Again, the quote can be identified by centre, e.g.:
LIBOR – London interbank offered rate;
SIBOR – Singapore interbank offered rate.

Note:

(a) Rates are quoted bid/offer, it being more expensive to borrow than to deposit; therefore the offered rate is the higher of the two, e.g.:

Quoted interbank rates		Periods		
Financial centre	Overnight (O/N)	1 month	3 months	6 months
London	$10-10\frac{1}{8}$	$11-11\frac{1}{8}$	$10\frac{3}{8}-10\frac{1}{2}$	$10\frac{1}{4}-10\frac{3}{8}$
Zurich	$\frac{7}{8}-1$	$3\frac{7}{16}-3\frac{9}{16}$	$3\frac{1}{2}-3\frac{5}{8}$	$3\frac{3}{4}-3\frac{7}{8}$
Frankfurt	3.80–3.90	3.65–3.80	3.80–3.95	3.90–4.10
Paris	$9\frac{5}{16}-9\frac{3}{8}$	$8\frac{3}{8}-8\frac{1}{2}$	$8\frac{3}{8}-8\frac{1}{2}$	$8\frac{1}{2}-8\frac{5}{8}$

(b) Taking the Frankfurt overnight quote of 3.80–3.90 implies that the bank will pay interest at 3.80% to a bank or customer depositing funds with it. In the interbank market it will lend these funds at

3.90%. To lend funds to a customer of the bank, it will add on a margin to increase the lending rate to, say, 4.15%, a margin of 25 basis points.

Bid/offer spread

This is the margin to the bank between buying (bidding) and selling (offering) funds in the interbank market; e.g. a quote 10–10$\frac{1}{8}$ implies a $\frac{1}{8}$% spread margin to the bank. The spread will be affected by the bank's own position as to whether it wishes to bid and hence offer funds. The typical spread is 10–15 basis points.

Basis point

This is one hundredth part of 1%; 1,000 bp = 1.00%, therefore 12.5 bp = 0.00125, 0.125% or $\frac{1}{8}$%.

Long position

This occurs when a bank has excess funds, at which time it may reduce its bid rate below the market level in order not to attract depositors. It may also reduce its offered rate to attract borrowers in order to be able to bring its position into balance again.

Short position

In this case a bank lacks funds to lend. As a result it will increase its bid rate to attract depositors until the position is in balance again.

Note: A bank may decide deliberately to go long or short of funds in order to take advantage of anticipated changes in the yield curve. If rates are expected to rise the bank will bid aggressively for funds, which as the offered rate rises it can lend out at an increased marginal profit to itself.

Square position

This is a balanced position; 'the book is square' implies loans = deposits. There is no mismatch.

Yield

Yield is the interest rate return on deposits from an investor's viewpoint. It is the interest rate payable on loans from the borrower's viewpoint.

Yield curve

The shape of the yield curve is seen by plotting the LIBID or LIBOR rates against time.

Note: The yield curve has three basic shapes, depending on market perceptions for the future:

(a) Normal yield curve (Fig. 7.1), where long-term rates are more expensive than short-term rates. In this instance the market assumes additional risk attached to the length of time the funds are outstanding. If depositing, the investor will seek compensation for this risk, which the borrower is thus required to pay.

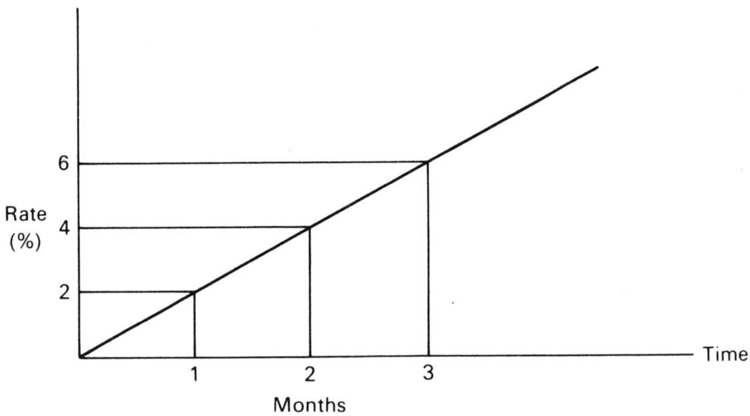

Fig. 7.1 Normal yield curve.

(b) Flat yield curve (Fig. 7.2), where the market perceives no additional risk over time. This may be typically seen in period rates with

Fig. 7.2 Flat yield curve.

maturities up to one year. It is more rare to see a flat yield curve over a number of years. In the Swiss and German markets the curve may be nearly flat since traditionally there have been few changes in the structure of their rates, a feature of this being low inflation in the two countries.

(c) Inverted yield curve: (Fig. 7.3), where long-term rates are lower than short-term rates. The investor is still encouraged to lend over the longer term, in the belief that short-term rates will fall substantially and the yield curve will to return to 'normal'.

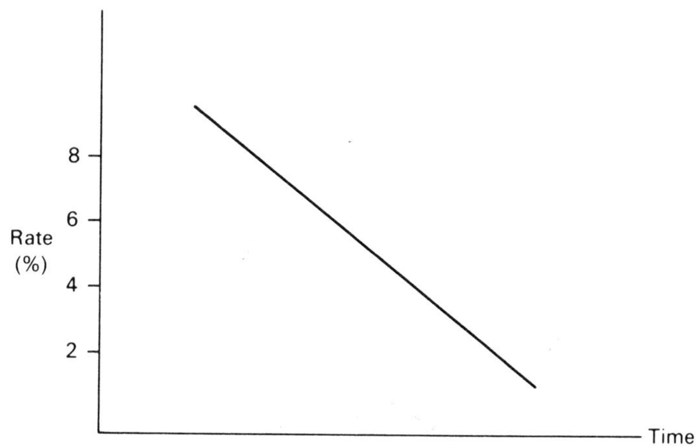

Fig. 7.3 Inverted yield curve.

Fixed rate

The interest rate is set at the beginning of the loan period for continuation of the loan until maturity, although interest may accrue and be paid at regular intervals throughout the loan period.

Floating rate

The interest rate is set at the beginning of the loan period and is applicable to that period only. Interest is paid at the end of the period. On maturity a new interest rate is fixed for the next loan period and so forth until the maturity date of the loan facility. Many such facilities will allow the borrower to repay and redraw funds throughout the term, or tenor, of the facility.

Tenor or term

This is the length of time that a loan facility is operative and can be utilised by the borrower.

Domestic interest rates

These are interest rates quoted in the base currency of a country, e.g. sterling rates in the United Kingdom, Deutschmark rates in West Germany, etc.

Euro interest rates

These are interest rates quoted in a foreign currency relative to the country, e.g. sterling rates in France, Deutschmark rates in the United Kingdom.

Note: The Euromarket came into existence after 1945. As a result of aid programmes to Europe, principally the Eastern bloc, large reserves of US dollars built up outside the United States. These would naturally have been held in the United States. However, due to the cold war, the Eastern countries in particular feared expropriation of their funds. It was then that they began to deposit US dollars in London, thereby immediately switching the legal liability from the United States.

Further impetus was given to the market as regulations were introduced in domestic markets to control domestic banking systems and currencies by exchange controls. Reserve requirements were set, as were restrictions on foreign capital movements. As these controls could only apply domestically, two markets in the same currency evolved – domestic and Euromarket.

The common factors where Eurocurrencies are traded are an acceptable political risk, no regulation affecting the cost of deposits or borrowings, and no restrictions on the inflow or outflow of currencies. Examples of the two rates are as follows:

	Domestic rates			Euro rates		
Period	£	DM	US$ Bankers' acceptances	£	DM	US$ Money market
1 month	$9\frac{15}{16}$	3.75	6.25	$9\frac{13}{16}$	$3\frac{13}{16}$	$6\frac{5}{16}$
2 months	$9\frac{7}{8}$	3.75	6.30	$9\frac{3}{4}$	$3\frac{13}{16}$	$6\frac{3}{8}$
3 months	$9\frac{13}{16}$	3.75	6.35	$9\frac{11}{16}$	$3\frac{13}{16}$	$6\frac{7}{16}$
6 months	$9\frac{5}{8}$	3.80	6.375	$9\frac{7}{16}$	$3\frac{13}{16}$	$6\frac{9}{16}$

Interest

Interest can accrue in different ways. Certain instruments in the market are always quoted in a certain manner.

Note: Interest accrual can be simple, annualised, compounded or on a discount basis. It may be quoted on a 360-day or 365-day basis, depending on the currency in question.

(a) Simple interest, or flat interest, does not take account of time; for example, 5% of 100 = 5. In this instance the 5% flat rate is always simply 5% of the amount in question. The formula for flat interest is:

$$\text{Amount} \times \frac{\text{Percentage rate}}{100}$$

$$\text{Therefore } \frac{100}{100} \times 5 = 5$$

(b) Annualised interest is simple interest with the time element factored in. For instance, if 5% in example (a) above was the applicable rate for three months, the annualised rate would be 20%, being:

$$\frac{12 \text{ months}}{3 \text{ months}} = 4$$

Therefore 5% for 3 months × 4 = 20% for one year. The formula for calculating interest is:

$$\text{Amount} \times \frac{\text{Per annum percentage rate}}{100} \times \frac{\text{Period (months or days)}}{\text{Year}}$$

$$\text{Therefore } 100 \times \frac{20}{100} \times \frac{3}{12} = 5$$

The denominator of the year can be expressed in months (12) or in days. In the sterling money market the convention is a 365-day year; however, in the dollar base and bond markets the convention is a 360-day year. Most currency money markets operate on a 360-day year, the exceptions being Belgium and Australia.

At the end of the loan the borrower will repay the principal plus interest, i.e. 100 + 5 = 105.

(c) Compound interest and discount interest refer to the timing of the interest payment. If interest is paid at the end of a loan it is called a balloon payment. If it is paid at the beginning of the loan it is called a discount, and if paid at intervals during the life of the loan it is said to be compound.

(i) Discount interest is an annualised rate but the interest is paid at the beginning of the loan period. As interest is paid up front, the effective rate of the loan will be different from the annualised rate:

$$\text{Principal amount} \times \frac{\text{Per annum percentage rate}}{100} \times \frac{\text{Period}}{\text{Year}}$$

$$100 \times \frac{20}{100} \times \frac{3}{12} = 5$$

With interest paid immediately the borrower will receive only $100-5 = 95$, but will have to pay 100 at the maturity of the loan. The effective rate of the loan can therefore be calculated as:

$$\frac{\text{Amount}}{\text{Principal amount}} \times \frac{\text{Period}}{\text{Year}} \times 100$$

$$\frac{95}{100} \times \frac{3}{12} \times 100 = 23.75\%$$

Thus 23.75% represents the effective or true annualised rate of borrowing 100, discounted at a rate of 20% for a period of three months.

(ii) Compound interest occurs where interest is calculated at intervals during the loan; it is known as interest on interest. For instance, a loan of 100 runs for three months at 20% per annum, on which interest is 5; however, the interest is not paid but added to the principal of 100 to total 105. Interest continues to be calculated for the next three-month period at 20% per annum. However, the principal amount of the loan on which interest will be calculated is 105. As a result the interest due at the end of six months is 5.25.

In total on the original loan of 100, interest of 10.25 will have been paid. Again, a true or effective rate of borrowing can be calculated:

$$\frac{\text{Total interest paid}}{\text{Principal loan}} \times \frac{\text{Year}}{\text{Period}} \times 100$$

$$\frac{10.25}{100} \times \frac{12}{6} \times 100 = 20.5\%$$

Thus 20.5% represents the effective or true annualised rate of borrowing 100 for six months where interest of 20% has been compounded three-monthly.

MANAGING THE EXPOSURE

A company is subject to interest rate exposure whether it has surplus funds to invest, i.e. it is 'long' of cash, or whether it has a requirement for funds and is therefore a borrower, i.e. 'short' of cash.

The exposure arises in the fluctuation of interest rates over the time period that the company is either 'long' or 'short' of funds. In the end, it depends on whether the company could have invested more wisely to earn a better return overall by having lent money for a shorter period as rates have increased and relent it to take account of the rate increase. The reverse is true in the context that if borrowing rates are increasing the borrower would seek to 'lock' in for a longer time period at the lower rate.

In each case it is the anticipation of the shape of the yield curve which leads a company to take a certain action, yet it is the reality of the yield curve over time against which a company is measured.

For example, a company investing for six months (Figs. 7.4 and 7.5) takes the following action:

1. Invest for a one-month period.
2. End of the month, invest for a further month.
3. End of second month invest for a further month.
4. On deposit renewal invest until time that funds are required.

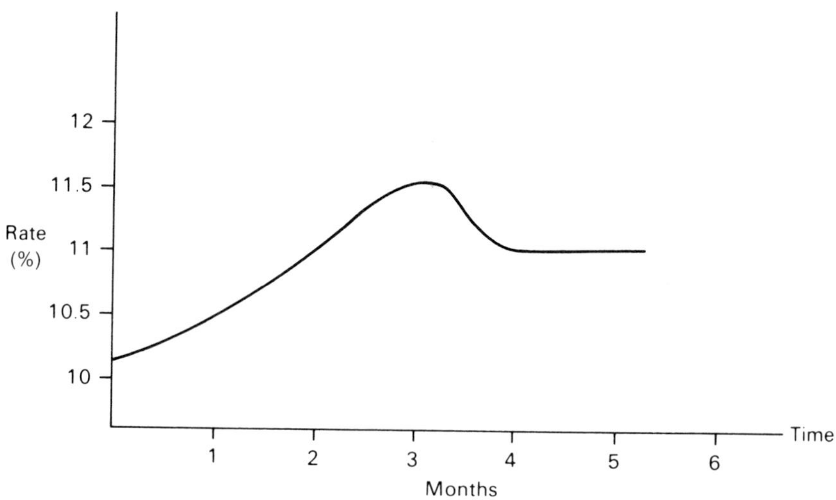

Fig. 7.4 Anticipated yield curve.

The following action should have been taken:

1. Initially the company should have invested for four months.
2. On renewal date invest for one month.
3. Finally invest for one further month, or until funds required.

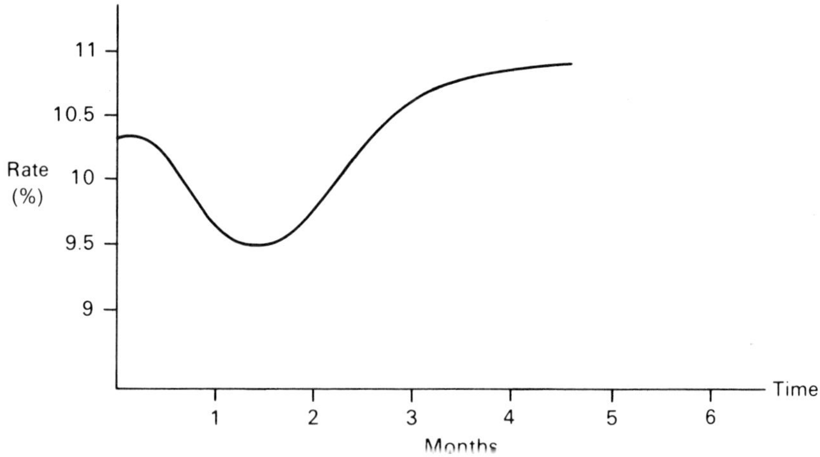

Fig. 7.5 Actual yield curve.

In reality a company would make a fresh decision on each rollover date of the investment, in the light of the then current circumstances. This gives the company the opportunity to revise its forecast yield curve.

Exactly the same decision process applies to the borrower in deciding what loan interest period to borrow for (Figs. 7.6 and 7.7). In this case the action taken is to borrow for six months, or until funds will be repaid from surplus cash.

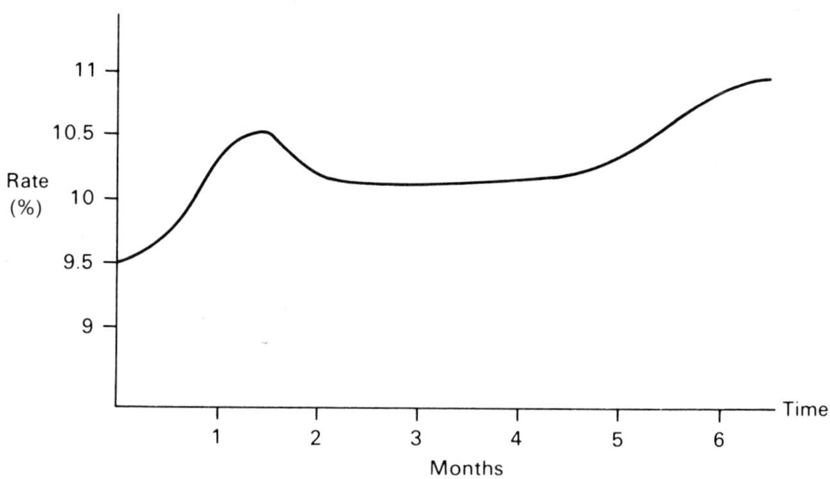

Fig. 7.6 Anticipated yield curve.

The following action should have been taken:

1. Borrow for one month.

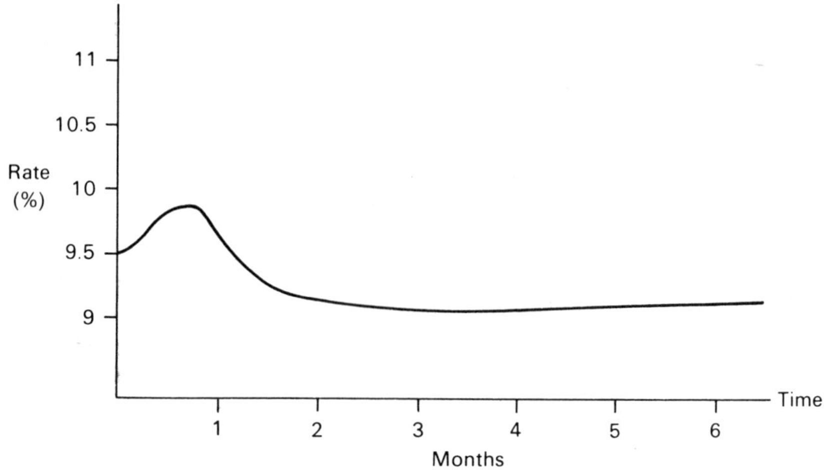

Fig. 7.7 Actual yield curve.

2. On renewal date borrow until funds to be repaid.

In this instance the borrower will have suffered a higher overall cost of borrowing by taking the action it did, i.e. six months at 9.5% versus one month at 9.5% plus five months at 9%.

These illustrations merely seek to prove how difficult it can be to make a decision in this field. The market does not work in a consistent manner and external causes can result in radical reassessments of the yield curve. Exposure management is therefore an art rather than a science, relying on the best guesstimate of the future on information available at the time.

There are various opportunities for a company in how it might borrow or invest funds. These opportunities could be described as the money market instruments, and are used for physically managing the exposure. However, there are methods available to the corporate cash manager to introduce flexibility into the borrowing or investment portfolio should circumstances change (the swap market), and lastly there are insurance-type arrangements which allow the corporate to limit its downside risk.

MONEY MARKET INSTRUMENTS

The borrower

Overdraft

This is the most commonly used form of borrowing. An overdraft is an agreed limit with the bank, up to which the company may borrow without further reference to the bank. The limit and the interest rate margin charged will be negotiated with the bank from time to time, depending (a) on the company's needs and (b) on its financial strength.

The funds drawn under an overdraft limit are on a revolving basis, i.e. if they are repaid they can be redrawn up to a maximum of the agreed limit. Technically the overdraft is a demand line, in that the bank can call for repayment at short notice. However, in practice the facilities tend to be negotiated on an annual basis.

Blue-chip or prime borrowers would tend to borrow at 1% per annum over the bank's base rate. This base rate is calculated by the banks with reference to current money market rates. As a result it fluctuates from time to time. Interest is payable quarterly or semi-annually and is calculated on a daily basis on the amount of borrowing outstanding. Within a company structure of many domestic subsidiaries or operating units, it is possible to structure one overdraft limit and sub-limits for each unit. Within this scheme interest may be set off without legal set-off on the loans and deposits themselves, which would be contra to any negative hedge clause the company may have in other loan agreements.

In diagrammatic form this would be as shown in Fig. 7.8.

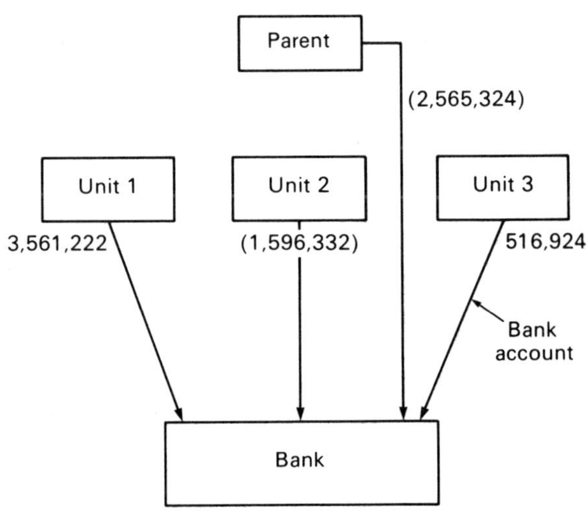

Fig. 7.8 Company overdraft scheme.

Each unit, including the parent, would have a bank account and limit with the bank under an overall overdraft limit of, say, £5 million. Example balances are marked, on any one day:

Unit	£
Unit 1	3,561,222
Unit 2	(1,596,332)
Unit 3	516,924
Parent	(2,565,324)
Net sum overdrawn:	(83,510)

If the rate (including margin) was 12%, the net interest payable by the group on this day would be:

$$83{,}510 \times \frac{12}{100} \times \frac{1}{365} = £(27.45)$$

Each unit in overdraft would pay interest on its outstanding balance of 12%, while those in credit would get the benefit of earning interest at 12%. The latter is of course significantly better than would be available on money market deposit. Therefore each company would pay/receive:

Unit	£
Unit 1	1,170.81
Unit 2	(524.82)
Unit 3	169.95
Parent	(843.39)
Net:	(27.45)

In this instance the benefit of the set-off arrangement accrues to each unit, and is therefore an incentive for it to be in surplus funds. However, for tax reasons, as this situation is artificial, the interest earned rate may have to be reduced to be more in line with market rates. At that point the benefit would accrue to the parent because through the netting system, in co-operation with the bank, it would be allocating interest income and expense. Therefore it is allocating the full cost of interest, but by reducing the units' earned interest income the balance would be kept at the centre. Supposing interest was charged at 12% but the investment rate was only 11%. The 1% differential (£111.73) would remain at the centre as additional income.

Unit		£
Unit 1		1,073.25
Unit 2		(524.82)
Unit 3		155.78
Parent	(843.39)	
	111.73	(731.66)
Net:		(27.45)

The overdraft is the most flexible form of short-term borrowing. It is a widely available instrument in Europe, Canada and Australia, but is not technically available in the United States – although banks there can arrange swing line facilities for a borrower, which seeks to serve the same purpose.

Money market

The short-term money market is highly liquid for maturities up to two years, though in the larger money centres around the world this is being stretched to five years.

The market is not a physical exchange but rather a loose collection of brokers, banks, institutions and corporates, all communicating mainly by telephone or electronically and via telex and telefax machines. The depth and breadth of the money market in a financial centre in part rests on the tax regime of the country; usually traditional links with commodity trading; and the willingness of the authorities to allow registration, or granting of licences, to a wide variety of organisations. Central banks and authorities in general are stringent in their analysis before permitting organisations to take deposits, and strictly apply continuing monitoring and compliance criteria.

In simplistic terms the market is split between the professionals dealing with each other, known as the interbank market, and the corporate market, where banks and brokers deal with corporates. 'Money market' tends to imply short-term deposits or borrowings but in reality all transactions, whether of a long-, short- or medium-term nature, are traded through the market in either cash terms or paper terms. The money markets in a sense incorporate the exchange markets too since any currency, subject to its domestic exchange controls, can be borrowed or deposited in a money market.

Banks will quote rates to corporates on a bid and offer basis related to the then current LIBID and LIBOR rates. So for a borrower wishing to borrow, say, £5 million for three months, the bank would quote an all-in price comprising LIBOR plus the borrower's margin. The margin represents the return to the bank for taking on a risk associated with lending to that customer.

The margin may differ for a customer between its committed facilities, where the margins are negotiated and documented, and uncommitted facilities or advised lines, where the all-in rate quoted is dependent on a combination of the bank's position and market conditions. When a company deals through a broker it will be charged a commission for so doing, typically $\frac{1}{16}$th on the face value of the borrowing.

A borrower should seek a balanced portfolio between short-, medium-

and long-term borrowing. The relationship between each will depend on the nature of the company. For instance, a manufacturing company that is capital-intensive will probably have borrowed funds biased in the medium- and long-term. A retail service company, on the other hand, will likely be needing funds only for working capital and will concentrate on short-term funding. Such a mix in the portfolio is also a natural hedge against movement in the yield curve.

Borrowing in the money market is simple and straightforward; however, it may not always be the most cost-effective instrument and some analysis should be undertaken to gauge whether the borrowing should be by way of overdraft or in a foreign currency swapped into the base currency.

Calculation of overdraft break-even rate. This seeks to set a target rate between borrowing overnight on overdraft, or in the money market. The equation takes into account the interest on interest factor. Overdraft interest is calculated on the daily outstanding balance until the interest is paid, either quarterly or semi-annually.

$$\frac{\text{Overdraft rate}}{\left[\dfrac{\text{Overdraft rate}\left[\begin{array}{l}\text{Days remaining}\\ \text{to interest}\\ \text{payment date}\end{array} - \text{Days loan period}\right]}{365 \times 100}\right]} + 1$$

For example:
Overdraft rate 10.5%
Days until interest payment date 87
Days loan period 1

$$\frac{10.5}{\left[\dfrac{10.5\,[87-1]}{36{,}500}\right]} + 1 = \frac{10.5}{\left[\dfrac{903}{36{,}500}\right]} + 1 = \frac{10.5}{0.0247} + 1 = \frac{10.5}{1.0247}$$

$$\underline{\underline{10.2469}}$$

In this instance this implies that if money market rates on overnight borrowing are less than 10.2469% then they should be taken, but if the rate quoted is, say, 10.375% it should be rejected in favour of the overdraft. The formula does not cover all the costs such as telephone, confirmations, etc., associated with a deal so the break-even rate should be adjusted slightly. To underpin the target by $\frac{1}{2}\%$ on a borrowing of £500,000 would 'save' the interest cost of £6.85 on an overnight borrowing. This would go some way to covering the associated dealing costs. If the borrowing was more substantial, say £5,000,000, the saving would be £68.49.

This simple methodology can be used as a bench-mark in monitoring the performance of the cash management function (see Chapter 10).

Calculation of an effective cost of borrowing. This combines the money and foreign exchange markets. It can be used to calculate the equivalent borrowing rate in the base currency after borrowing foreign currency and selling it spot for the base currency, while simultaneously buying back the foreign currency to meet the obligation of repaying the loan plus interest.

$$\frac{365}{\text{Number of Days}}\left[\frac{\text{Spot rate}}{\text{Forward rate}}\left\{1+\frac{\text{Borrowing rate of currency}\times\text{Number of days}}{360}\right\}-1\right]\times 100$$

Note: The spot rate is the rate for selling currency for the base currency. The forward rate is the outright rate for selling the base currency for the currency. The borrowing rate is: $\frac{\text{Rate}}{100}$.

For example:

Number of days	180
Spot rate	1.5125
Forward rate	1.5400
Borrowing rate	6.5%, i.e. 0.065

$$\frac{365}{180}\left[\frac{1.5125}{1.5400}\left\{1+\frac{0.065\times 180}{360}\right\}-1\right]\times 100$$

$$2.03\ [0.9821\ \{1.0325\}-1]\times 100$$

$$2.03\times 0.0140182\times 100 = 2.85\%$$

This implies that, borrowing in this way, the effective cost of borrowing the sterling amount would be 2.85% for six months. This rate should be compared with the calculation of the six-months break-even rate. If the effective rate is lower than the break-even rate, the company should borrow through the short-dated currency swap.

'Paper' market. An alternative to straight overdraft or money market borrowing is for the company to sell its 'paper'. This is in the form of selling a promise to pay at a future date, as detailed on a paper note. These paper markets fall into two categories: the acceptance market and the commercial paper market.

Acceptance market. The instrument in the acceptance market is called an acceptance credit. It is very similar in nature to a bill of exchange, the difference being that an acceptance credit is a bill of exchange drawn by a company on a bank rather than on another company.

A company, under an acceptance credit facility from a bank, will draw a bill on the bank. The bank will accept this, thereby promising to pay out the amount of the bill at some future date, the maturity date. The bank will pay to the company the discounted proceeds of the face value of the acceptance, at a rate in line with market rates and inclusive of a margin. The bank may decide to onsell the bill to another bank or discount house, or indeed hold it to maturity. On maturity the company pays the bank the face value of the bill.

The rate offered by the accepting bank in sterling acceptances will be slightly affected by whether it is eligible or non-eligible at the Bank of England. An eligible bill implies that the bank can place the bill at the Bank of England as part of the reserve assets it is required to hold. As a consequence, eligible bank bills tend to be less expensive than non-eligible bills.

The documentation and operation of an acceptance credit line is simple. As before, the acceptance rate will be compared with the break-even rate in the decision process of whether to issue acceptances.

In the US market there are more stringent rules in the monitoring and clausing of bills. In London the clausing – the reason for borrowing shown on the face of the bill – tends to be general, as this form of finance is widely used for working capital rather than specifically for trade purposes. In the United States the information requirement is more precise, the intention being to state clearly that finance is required for trade purposes.

Commercial paper market. In these markets the company issues paper direct to the market through a bank acting as its agent (dealer). The paper, each note, is basically a promise to pay the face value of the note on its maturity date.

The main commercial paper markets are the following:

1. US commercial paper market (US$CP). This is a domestic commercial

paper market, though foreign issuers are allowed to participate. An issuer has to be rated by at least two reputable rating agencies in New York before any paper may be offered for sale to investors through a dealer. The two notable rating agencies are Moody's and Standard and Poors. One of the criteria of the rating process, apart from the strength and track record of the company, is the inclusion of back-up lines. The rationale is that if the commercial paper market collapsed, the company must have sufficient funds or access to other funds to repay notes outstanding and to continue the financing of the company. The paper is sold to or placed with professional investors, pension funds, corporates and institutions by a dealer (an investment bank). The dealer will issue an information memorandum on the issuer to its clients, the potential investors. That memorandum will detail the company's business and performance. It is unlike a broker's memorandum in that the dealer is not recommending to investors that they should buy the paper. The investor will have tight investment criteria as to the types of paper it can invest in, largely based on the ratings issued by the rating agencies mentioned above. The other party involved in the issuance is the issuing and paying agent, who physically fills in the details on the notes as they are issued, collects the funds at the time of issuance and arranges repayment at the time of maturity. Notes are issued in minimum denominations of US$100,000 up to a maximum maturity of 270 days and they are sold at a discount, the funds generally being used for working capital purposes. There is no secondary market as such, though a dealer to an issue may purchase paper for its own inventory.

2. Euro-commercial paper market (ECP). This is the issuance of currency-denominated paper in a market other than that of the country of the currency – for instance, Eurodollar commercial paper issued in London. Issuance is centred on London although the paper is traded globally. The method of issuing and selling paper is similar to that in the US commercial paper market. However, it is not required that the paper be rated, and a wider range of banks act as dealers. The market itself is more name-related, as is the Eurobond market in general, though ratings will likely become the norm in the commercial paper market. In the early days of the market, paper was issued on a tender panel basis and underwritten. The tender panel, a group of banks, would bid for the paper to be issued by the company. The company would issue to those members of the panel offering the most competitive rates. This was backed up by the banks' agreement to underwrite the issuance of any paper if any tender panel members did not take up their allotments. This system is cumbersome as extra days

have to be allowed for tender panel members to bid for the paper; it was common for the process to take five days. In volatile markets, rates bid five days prior to issuance could be markedly different from those prevailing on the issuance day. As a result, and also because the market has grown in depth and breadth, it is now more usual for an issuer to appoint two or three dealers. This has shortened the issuance notice period to two days. The issuer can also put up existing facilities as backstop lines to negate the need for underwriting from dealers and in turn save costs. Most issuers are in the position that if their paper cannot be sold, or it is too expensive at a particular time, they will resort to the money market for any cash required. If this market too is inaccessible, the issuer will call on its committed facilities from the banks. Like the US$CP market, ECP is sold on a discount basis. There is also an issuing paying agent, with settlement through Cedel or Euroclear. At present the ECP market is predominantly dollar-based, though other currencies on the Euro-basis are beginning to be issued. There is more active secondary market in paper, and maturities tend to be longer than in the US$CP market.

3. Sterling commercial paper market (SCP). This market was established in 1986 in London as a domestic market. While there is no requirement for rating at present, there are certain criteria on issuance laid down by the Bank of England. The issuer must be a publicly quoted company (or a subsidiary thereof) on The Stock Exchange, with net assets of £50 million. The minimum maturity is seven days, with a maximum of 364 days. The issues can be direct to investors but are more typically via dealers. Underwriting is not a requirement. Like the other commercial paper markets, the notes are in bearer form and are issued at a discount. Initially issuers used the tender panel mechanism to price notes, but this is giving way to dual or triple dealership arrangements, as in the ECP market. When the market originally opened it was thought that it would imply the collapse of the acceptance market. However, this has not been the case.

There are other commercial paper markets in centres around the world: Australia, France, The Netherlands and Hong Kong, to name a few. The characteristics of these markets are in general similar to those noted above.

The investor

Current account

This tends to be an ineffective method of investing funds because banks are not geared to paying interest on such accounts. Any interest paid is usually a token amount. It is therefore more efficient for a company to maintain its current account at a minimal overdraft level and to invest surplus funds elsewhere.

In the United Kingdom the lack of sophistication in placing deposits has for many years funded the banks' ability to lend. However, with increased awareness and competition the opportunity for a bank to rely on 'free' balances has gone. In most instances banks will pay a percentage of their base rate as deposit interest, normally on a semi-annual basis.

By contrast, in the United States the corporate investor has for many years had a greater awareness and wider opportunity, by virtue of the number of different short-term instruments available for investing surplus funds.

Money market

As for the borrower, the money market is an easy market for the investor to access. The players are the same. In investing funds it is difficult to set a bench reference rate, similar to that of the break-even overdraft rate on borrowings. In one sense the current account rate can be taken, but it is not a true market rate and is therefore not comparable. Also, as previously stated, it is not an efficient method of depositing funds.

The market bench-mark rate for deposits in London for any currency is LIBID, The London Interbank Bid Rate. LIBID is generally quoted, though it may differ from bank to bank depending on the bank's own position. For example, a foreign bank that does not have ready natural access to sterling funds will tend to bid aggressively for deposits. It will thus quote a higher bid rate than, say, one of the clearers with its domestic retail network which supplies sterling, therefore making it an investor of sterling itself.

In depositing funds the investor seeks security, yield and liquidity.

Security. This is all-important, in order to ensure that funds will be repaid on the due date. To this end the company should maintain an internal list of institutions with which it will deposit funds, and up to what amounts. This is an important element of control (see Chapter 9). The list should be reviewed regularly.

Yield. The investor is looking for a beneficial yield to improve the return on the funds invested. That expected yield should be compared with alternative instruments available, bearing in mind the relative security aspects. Higher yields would tend normally to indicate higher attendant risks.

Liquidity. The requirement by an investor for liquidity will be a factor of internal forecasting; for instance, the funds may be *known* to be required at a future date, or they *may* be required. In the latter case, flexibility and liquidity would be more important. Flexibility can be achieved more readily in the paper markets than in the money markets, because in the latter there is a cost of breaking a fixed deposit with an institution, while in the former where there is a secondary market the paper can be sold on.

It is basically these three factors that will influence the investor. There are other considerations, such as tax, which will vary with the instruments and should be checked individually. The investor should aim to balance the portfolio between short-, medium- and long-term investments. The extent of the mix will be dictated by the company's requirements and the hedge it needs against possible changes in the yield curve.

The investor can therefore place cash deposits through brokers (the borrower on the other side of the transaction will pay the broker's commission), direct to bankers, or through the purchase of paper from dealers. The paper it can buy will be either commercial paper (being the other side of the mechanism mentioned earlier), certificates of deposit issued by banks and building societies in the United Kingdom, or floating rate notes, a form of longer-dated commercial paper.

Paper instruments

Certificates of deposit (CDs) are negotiable interest-bearing certificates evidencing a time deposit at a bank. CDs are issued by banks in certain countries in their domestic currencies. Euro-CD markets exist in US dollars, Canadian and Australian dollars, the yen, and the basket of currencies of the SDR (Special Drawing Rights) and ECU (European Currency Unit). An Asian dollar CD market operates in the Far East.

In the United Kingdom CDs are issued by banks and building societies. The CD is issued in minimum note size of £50,000 up to a maximum of £1,000,000. The notes are issued at par on an interest-to-maturity basis for periods of between 28 days and five years. Interest is paid on maturity of issues of less than one year, and annually on issues over one year.

Eurodollar CDs are issued in multiples of US$1,000 from a minimum of US$25,000. Typical note size is US$1,000,000. The interest payment dates are similar to those of sterling CDs, though interest is calculated on a 360-day year rather than the 365-day year for sterling.

CDs are usually issued at a fixed rate for the maturity, although there are floating rate certificates of deposit (FRCDs).

Certificates of deposit and floating rate notes (FRNs) are normally issued for longer periods than commercial paper, so the secondary markets are more developed. An investor will buy a primary or secondary note, i.e. a note at issuance (primary) or one at any stage prior to maturity (secondary). As interest is payable only on set dates, in buying a CD or FRN – except on original issuance or a rate-fixing date for an FRN – the investor has to compensate the seller by paying the interest accrued to date on the instrument.

The formula applied to sterling CDs with a maturity of less than one year is as follows:

$$\text{Principal amount} \times \frac{(365 \times 100) + \left(\text{Interest rate on CD} \times \text{Total tenor in days of CD at issue}\right)}{(365 \times 100) + \left(\text{Yield to maturity at which CD is purchased} \times \text{Days remaining of CD until maturity}\right)}$$

$$= \text{Proceeds received by depositor}$$

For example, a depositor purchases a sterling CD of face value £100,000 with a maturity of 90 days at a rate of $9\frac{7}{8}\%$ per annum. The depositor wishes to sell the sterling CD after 50 days. In the market the quote for the CD was $9\frac{5}{8}\%$–$9\frac{3}{4}\%$; using the formula above:

$$100{,}000 \times \frac{(36{,}500) + (9.875 \times 90)}{(36{,}500) + (9.75 \times 40)} = \text{Proceeds}$$

$$100{,}000 \times \frac{37{,}388.75}{36{,}890.00} = \text{Proceeds}$$

$$100{,}000 \times 1.0135199 = £101{,}351.99$$

In this instance the depositor is forgoing a higher yield to maturity as rates have fallen, and picking up on the cash benefit immediately. Therefore, to calculate the actual yield the depositor obtained on the CD:

$$\text{Yield to the depositor} = 100 \frac{(\text{Actual income})}{\text{Face amount of CD} \times \dfrac{\text{Number of days CD held}}{365}}$$

$$Y = 100 \frac{(1{,}351.99)}{\dfrac{(100{,}000 \times 50)}{365}} = 9.8695\%$$

However, as can be seen the depositor would have made a loss on the yield by selling before maturity of:

$$9.875 - 9.8695 = 0.0055\%$$

This is obviously not always the case, and the situation would have to be recalculated on each occasion to decide whether the CD should be sold. On some occasions it would be more beneficial to borrow short-term to meet any shortfall rather than to sell the CD.

FLEXING THE PORTFOLIO

In the past, once a company had decided to cover its interest rate exposure in a certain way, whether on a fixed- or variable-rate basis, it was costly for it to 'change its mind' and break the commitment made to the bank. However, with the development of the swap market this is no longer the case.

A swap is an agreed exchange with a counterparty of a stream of payments or receipts calculated on a notional principal amount. There may or may not be an exchange of principal at the beginning and end of the arrangement. The counterparty is typically a bank, acting as an intermediary to alleviate credit risk problems for its clients. Originally, swaps were set up as means for a counterparty to raise money, on a fixed or floating basis, less expensively than by going to the market in its own right. The structure would be as illustrated in Fig. 7.9.

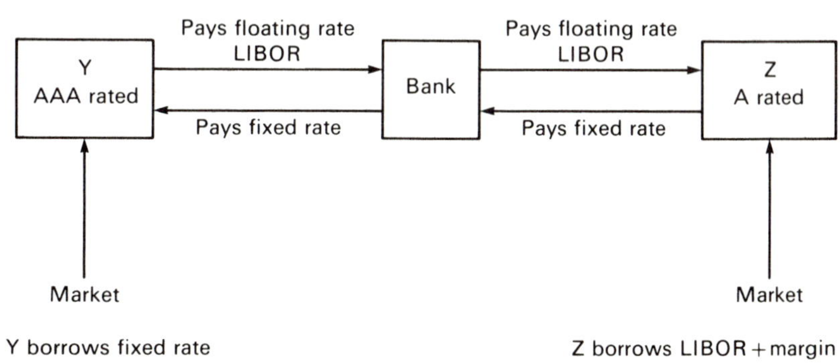

Fig. 7.9 Structure of a swap.

In this instance Z, an 'A' rated company, could not raise fixed funds as cheaply as Y company, which is 'AAA' rated; Y, however, in raising floating-rate funds, has to pay a margin over LIBOR. Therefore, in order to compensate Y for raising the fixed-rate issue, Z agrees to receive LIBOR flat, i.e. with no margin from Y, in return paying a fixed-rate coupon on its borrowing. Z's position, even after factoring in the cost of the margin in the LIBOR financing it still has to pay, has in effect created a fixed-rate loan at a cheaper cost.

This situation has been extended in its use to cover interest rate management of existing flows of interest rather than necessarily creating new flows. The principle, in essence, is still the same.

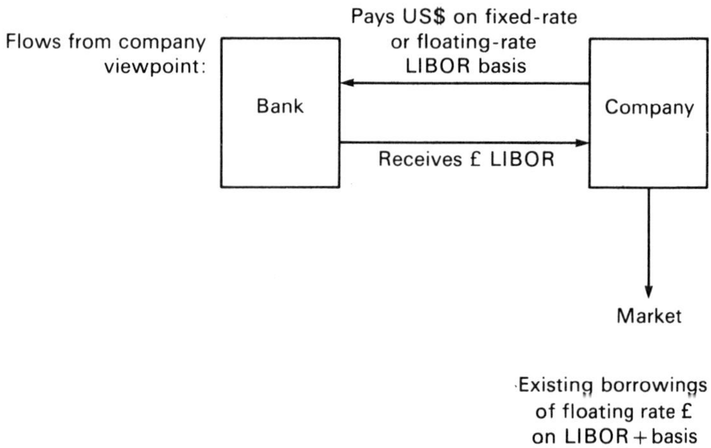

Fig. 7.10 Coupon or interest rate swap.

In the 'traded' swaps market the bank acts as counterparty and will take on a swap position, which it will arbitrage out of by finding suitable counterparties at a later date. The preparedness of the banks to take swap positions has led to the coupon swaps being traded like money market instruments, whereas currency coupon swaps tend still to be bespoke.

A coupon swap or interest rate swap is where the interest flows in the same currency, fixed for floating or vice versa, are swapped (see Fig. 7.10).

A currency coupon swap or currency interest rate swap has the additional feature of two currencies being involved (see Fig. 7.11).

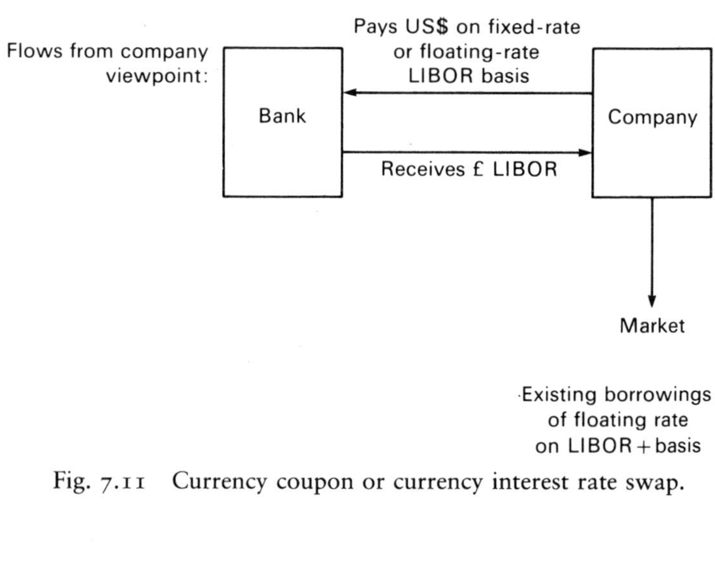

Fig. 7.11 Currency coupon or currency interest rate swap.

Swaps can be entered into to manage both liability and asset positions, in one currency or two. Therefore, if a company's views on the interest rate yield curve and currency relationship have changed, it can take advantage of this by swapping out of its original position into a new one.

For example, a company has US dollar fixed liabilities matching investment in the United States. The company's profile changes to become predominantly sterling-based with little US income. By entering into a swap the situation could be corrected (Fig. 7.12).

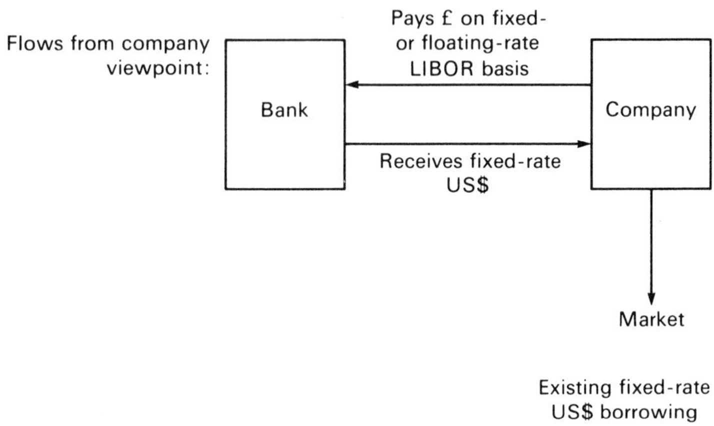

Fig. 7.12 Currency swap to correct liability position.

A swap would be based on current rates; therefore there might be a gain or loss to the company on the difference between the present cost of fixed-rate US dollars and that on the existing loan.

Asset swap flows would simply be the reverse of those stated, so that the company receives fixed or floating, and pays floating or fixed to match its receivables in the market (Fig. 7.13).

The swap product is extremely flexible, and is a useful tool in corporate cash management.

A swap can be cancelled by entering into the equal and opposite transaction or by receiving or paying the equivalent discounted cash flows of the future stream of receipts or payments.

The product itself is being developed to embrace options on swaps or 'swaptions', whereby for a premium a company has the right but not the obligation to enter into a swap at a future date. Swaps can be created to match a company's loan, maturity profile or project cycle. The possibilities come under the terms of financial engineering, where a particular problem may be resolved by using a combination of instruments.

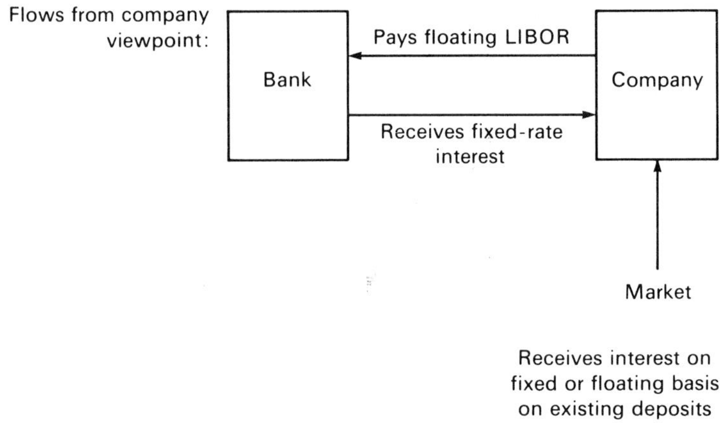

Fig. 7.13 Asset swap flow

INSURING THE PORTFOLIO (INTEREST RATE GUARANTEES)

There are certain products available which a company can use to 'insure' its loan or asset portfolio against adverse interest rate movements. These are through the futures market, forward forward contracts, forward rate agreements, interest rate options, or interest rate caps, floors or collars.

Futures market

The futures market is an exchange market. The main futures markets are located in Chicago, New York and London, with local markets in Sydney, Singapore, Montreal and Toronto.

A financial futures contract commits the parties involved to buy or sell a financial instrument of a specified quantity and quality at a future date. Contracts are traded by open outcry and are quoted on an index basis, with a price represented as 100 minus the implied interest rate for the instrument. The higher the interest rate, the lower the price of the future. (There are specific terms referred to in the futures market. Those most frequently used are listed on pages 179–80.) An example of an interest rate futures contract appears on the following page.

A company will use the futures market to offset its cash position; however, because the contracts traded are a standard size it is difficult for a corporate to hedge its position exactly. A second problem is that a futures position needs constant monitoring, and action when margin calls need to be funded. The cash management department would thus require

Exchange	IMM	LIFFE
Contract	Euro$ time deposit	3 month sterling interest rate
Unit of trading	US$1,000,000	£250,000
Contract standard face value	3 mth Euro$1 million by seller at cash settlement	3 mth £ deposit arranged designated bank name *or* cash settlement at buyer's option based on settlement price
Delivery months	Mar, June, Sept & Dec	Mar, June, Sept & Dec
Quotation	100 minus rate of interest in basis points	100 minus rate of interest in basis points
Minimum price		one basis point
Movement & value		£6.25
Price limit	100 basis points (US$2,500)	100 basis points (£625.00)
Initial margin		£500
Trading hours	7.30 a.m.–2.00 p.m. (Chicago time)	9.00 a.m.–3.02 p.m. (London time)

appropriate staffing. The following example illustrates the use of the futures market.

A company needs to raise £1,000,000 for three months. Anticipating a rise in interest rates, the company takes out a futures position. The time is now June, and expected payment date is September.

	Cash market	Futures market
June	Anticipate higher interest rates in September from 12%	Sell 4 (4 × £250,000) September contracts at 88 (12%)
Sept.	Borrow £1,000,000 in market at 16%	Buy 4 September contracts at 84

Result

Cash market £

Cost of loan increased from 12% to 16%

over 3 months $(1{,}000{,}000 \times \frac{4}{100} \times \frac{3}{12})$ = 10,000

Futures market

Profit of 400 (8,800 − 8,400) basis points at a value of £6.25 per basis point each contract (400 × 6.25 × 4) = 10,000

Net loss of interest = —

This situation ignores the cost of initial and maintenance margins. If interest rates had moved the other way, the cash and futures would have reacted accordingly and again the position would have netted out.

Forward forward contracts

These are specified agreements between a bank and its customer, and are tailored to the customer's requirements. In essence they commit the customer to borrow or deposit a set amount in the future for a specified period, at a rate fixed today.

For example, a company wishes to borrow £1,000,000 for three months in three months' time but fixing the rate for that borrowing today, because it anticipates interest rates will rise. This can be represented schematically as follows:

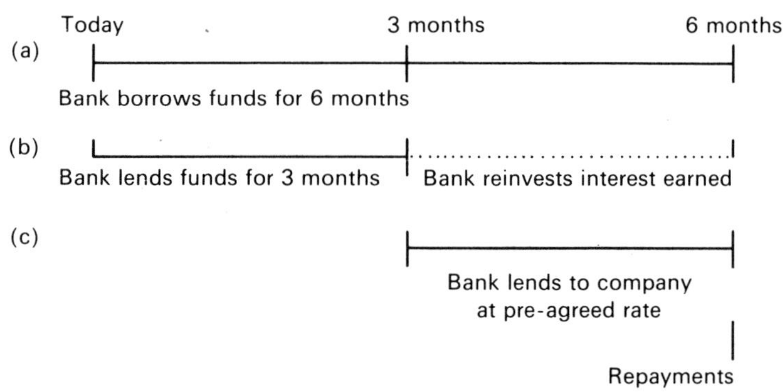

This formula uses interest rates expressed in decimals to calculate the break-even forward forward rate (RFF):

Notation:	P	= principal	1,000,000
	R_1	= rate applicable to shorter period	10.875
	R_2	= rate applicable to longer period	10.6875
	T_1	= time in days of shorter period	90
	T_2	= time in days of longer period	180
	I_1	= interest relating to shorter period	26,815.07
	I_2	= interest relating to longer period	52,705.48

$$RFF = \frac{365}{T_2 - T_1}\left[\frac{\frac{R_2\,T_2}{365} - \frac{R_1\,T_1}{365}}{1 + \left\{\frac{R_1\,T_1}{365}\right\}}\right]$$

$$RFF = \frac{365}{90}\left[\frac{\frac{19.2375}{365} - \frac{9.7875}{365}}{1 + \left\{\frac{9.7875}{365}\right\}}\right] = 4.06\left[\frac{0.0527 - 0.0268}{1 + (0.0268)}\right]$$

$$= 4.06 \left[\frac{0.0259}{1.0268}\right] = 4.06 \times 0.0252 = 0.102312 \times 100 = 10.2312$$

Forward rate agreements

These are agreements between a bank and its customer to compensate one another in cash for the movement of floating rates above or below a predetermined level for a future specified period. Since there is no movement of principal there is more flexibility in hedging interest rate risk than with a forward forward. However, there is still a commitment to undertake the compensation. It can be cancelled by reversing the FRA.

Interest rate options

The options market is normally reviewed in the context of currency options (see Chapter 8). However, there has been a growth in interest rate options as a means of limiting the downside risk from interest rate fluctuations. The cost of so doing is the premium of entering into the option. The options are traded on exchanges under set contract specifications.

For example, a company has a loan maturing in two months' time, at which point the six-month borrowing rate (the rollover rate) will be reset. Anticipating that the rates will rise, the company buys an option with a strike price of 10% and premium cost of 0.45%. At maturity there are three possibilities:

1. The rollover rate is 10% which, being the same as the strike price, will imply a loss to the company of its premium of 0.45%. This should be compared with having taken out an FRA or not hedging at all.
2. The rollover rate is higher, say 13%. In this case the company would exercise the option and be out of pocket on the premium of 0.45%.
3. The rollover rate is lower, say 8%. The option would be allowed to lapse, the cost being the premium of 0.45%. However, this is a better situation than with an FRA, because the company would have had to compensate the bank for the 2% interest differential.

Interest rate caps, floors and collars

These are an extension of the previously mentioned interest rate guarantee schemes.

Caps

An interest rate cap is a means of protection against rising short-term floating rates. In exchange for a premium the bank (or writer) undertakes to compensate the purchaser for any rise in rates above a specified rate for a specified period. This is a bespoke or over-the-counter interest rate option.

Floors

The floor is the opposite of a cap in that it seeks to protect against a fall in short-term interest rates. Again, it is basically an over-the-counter interest rate option, and a premium is paid.

Collars

These are a combination of caps and floors, creating a range of tolerance within which the company accepts any rise or fall of interest rates. Compensatory payments are made only when rates fall outside the range. The premium is much reduced because the company is also taking risk, and in some cases it is negated. The collar range can be specified by the company; or in setting an upper or lower level the bank will compute the other end of the range, based on volatility factors. This is called a range interest rate forward.

CHAPTER 8

Managing currency rate exposure

CHAPTER AIM

To understand the terminology and methodology of rate quotation in the spot and forward exchange markets; to understand the use and application of market techniques in managing exchange exposure.

QUOTATION OF RATES: SOME DEFINITIONS

Direct quotation

This is the amount of base currency required to purchase or sell one unit of foreign currency. For example, if 54.05 US cents would buy one Deutschmark, this would be a direct quote.

Indirect quotation

This is the amount of foreign currency required to purchase or sell one unit of base currency; e.g. 1.8500 Deutschmarks would buy one US dollar. *Note:* Most quotations are indirect and written as base currency/foreign currency, e.g. US$/DM. The direct quote is the reciprocal of the indirect.

Bid

The bid rate is the rate at which a bank will bid, or buy, a currency.

Offer

This is the rate at which a bank will offer, or sell, a currency.

Spread

Spread is the margin to the bank between the bid and offer rates. It is not a 'profit' but is to compensate the bank should it be unable to match a deal by buying and selling simultaneously. The spread will probably widen if a small parcel of currency is being traded or the market is volatile. The spread is usually expressed in terms of pips or points, e.g.:

Quote	Bid	Offer	Spread
US$/DM	1.8500	1.8510	10 pips (points)

Two-way price

This is a quote showing the bid and offer rates. Essentially each side of the quote is a price in itself, because as one currency is bought at the bid rate the bank is simultaneously selling the contra-currency at that rate. Taking the above example, the bid rate is 1.8500 where US dollars will be sold and the Deutschmarks bought. The offer rate is 1.8510 where US dollars will be bought and Deutschmarks sold.
Note: This interpretation is from the corporate viewpoint. A bank would take the reverse stance in buying US dollars at 1.8500 and selling US dollars at 1.8510.

Cross rate

This is the rate at which, by calculating two common rates, the third is quoted. For example:

(a) £/DM 2.8005

US$/DM 1.8500

$$\text{£/US\$} = \frac{2.8005}{1.8500} = 1.5138$$

(b) US$/DM 1.8500

£/US$ 1.5138

$$\text{£/DM} = 1.8500 \times 1.5138 = 2.8005$$

Note: As a rule of thumb where the common currency to the known quotes is the second element of the quotes, take the larger figure and divide by the smaller as in (a) above. Alternatively, where the common currency of the known quotes is diagonally positioned, as in (b) above, the figures should be multiplied.

Spot date

This refers to the date two business days hence.

Value date

This is the date at which currencies will be exchanged with value, i.e. available funds.
Note: The term 'for spot value' implies exchange will be in two business days' time. Spot value is typically the minimum period for exchanging currencies since traditionally it is the time taken for payment instructions in currencies to be acted upon and for cleared funds to be available. Nowadays, with electronic transfer mechanisms, some same-day exchanges can take place in US dollars versus the major currencies, depending on the capabilities of the bank.

Spot rate

The spot rate is the rate at which a bank will bid/offer currency for value two business days ahead.

Outright rate

This is the rate at which a bank will bid/offer currency at a future specified date.

Swap rate

This is the difference between the spot rate of a currency and its forward exchange rate. The pips, when added to or subtracted from the swap rate, give rise to the calculation of the outright rate.
Note: The pips (swap rate) are calculated based on the relative forward interest deposit rate differentials between the two currencies in question. This formula is as follows:

$$\frac{\text{Spot rate} \times \text{interest rate differential} \times \text{time}}{100 \times \text{time}}$$

e.g.:
Spot rate: £/US$ 1.5138
Time: 3 months
Interest rate differential: 3 month Euro £ deposit rate = 10.875%
3 month Euro $ deposit rate = 6.375% = 4.5%

Using the formula: $\dfrac{1.5138 \times 4.5 \times 3}{100 \times 12} = \dfrac{20.4363}{1200} = 0.0170$

This would typically be quoted as 170 pips. It is important therefore to remember that currencies are quoted to four decimal places (notable exceptions being the yen and Belgian franc). To calculate the outright rate the 170 pips would in this case be subtracted from the spot rate to give an outright rate of 1.4968:

$$\begin{array}{r} 1.5138 \\ -0.0170 \\ \hline 1.4968 \end{array}$$

The pips are subtracted because the pound is at a premium relative to the dollar, indicated by the forward interest rate being higher. If the reverse were true, the pound would be said to be at a discount and the pips would be added to the spot rate. For instance:

Spot rate: £/US$ 1.5138
Interest rate differentials: 3 month Euro £ deposit rate = 9.75%
3 month Euro $ deposit rate = 11.25% = 1.5%

Using the formula: $\dfrac{1.5138 \times 1.5 \times 3}{100 \times 12} = \dfrac{6.8121}{1200} = 0.0057$

The outright rate would be:

$$\begin{array}{r} 1.5138 \\ +\ 0.0057 \\ \hline 1.5195 \end{array}$$

Swap rates and outright rates are quoted two-way, like spot rates, indicating the buying and selling prices. When swap rates only are quoted, say 170/180, there is a rule of thumb to indicate whether the forward is at a premium or discount. If the second figure is higher than the first, the forward is at a discount and the pips should be added. Conversely, if the second figure is lower than the first, the forward is therefore at a premium and the pips should be subtracted. It should be noted that this is the European basis for referring to discount and premium; in North America the terminology is reversed.

It is possible, if the pips are known, to calculate the interest rate differential at the forward date by using the formula:

$$\frac{\text{Swap rate (pips)} \times 100 \times \text{time}}{\text{Spot rate} \times \text{time}}$$

Using the result of the previous examples:

(a) $\dfrac{0.0170 \times 100 \times 12}{1.5138 \times 3} = 4.5\%$

(b) $$\frac{0.0057 \times 100 \times 12}{1.5138 \times 3} = 1.5\%$$

MANAGING EXCHANGE EXPOSURE

Internal exchange exposure techniques were discussed in Chapter 6 but should be reviewed in line with the external techniques outlined below, as together they form the basis for a company to manage its currency exposures.

In any given situation a choice of hedging techniques will apply. In consequence each should be evaluated, and the appropriate technique chosen. As business situations can alter, and so also the relevant exposures, it is important to retain some flexibility wherever possible. This may predicate the hedging technique chosen if the likelihood of change is high. Alternatively, only a proportion of the risk may be covered.

The area of hedging techniques is itself ever-changing and developing with new methods of solving risk situations. This is particularly so since the expansion of the futures and options markets around the world, as banks will offset their risks of taking on corporate exposure through these markets. The list of techniques below is therefore not an exhaustive one but rather aims to detail those most widely available and their application.

Forward foreign exchange contracts

A known, or anticipated, future exposure can be hedged by buying or selling currency at an outright rate for the future date. The key aspects in this method of hedging are that the commitment is firm and for a specified date. If circumstances subsequently change there may be a loss to the company in extricating itself from a position.

The method of calculating an outright, as already described, is based on the forward interest rate differential of the two currencies involved, translated into pips, relative to the current spot rate. At the agreed value date the two currencies are exchanged. This is termed 'closing out' the contract. Until that time the contract is said to be 'open'.

The bank will monitor the total of open contracts outstanding on either a gross or net basis against the company's credit limit for open foreign exchange contracts. It is important therefore that the company does likewise. A gross basis of monitoring is where the total of currency purchases and sales are added together to establish the outstanding position. The net is where purchases and sales are netted. In addition, the banks will assign a delivery risk limit, which is the associated risk that a company will not pay the currency owed to the bank on the contract maturity date. This delivery risk may be the same as spot delivery risk limit, which is for spot currency transactions. For example:

	Base currency
Total aggregate (gross) spot and forward value date limits	150,000,000
Forward value delivery risk limit	25,000,000
Spot value date delivery risk limit	50,000,000

However, banks recognise that the real value of the risk is less than the face value of the contracts, so to calculate actual credit exposure risk to a particular company, a percentage is applied. This percentage will vary between institutions and with the current volatility of exchange markets, but is normally between 10% and 25%:

Actual exposure	Base currency
15% of total exchange limit	22.5m
Forward delivery limit	25.0m
	47.5m

The availability of forward rates is dependent on whether there is a forward market in that currency, and on its 'depth'. If there is little trading or liquidity in a particular market it is said to lack 'depth'.

In most major trading currencies there are strong forward markets with liquidity being affected only by market volatility. However, in certain Third World currencies, often termed 'exotics', this is not the case. In these instances it may not be possible to set a forward outright because the bank cannot be sure that the local currency will be available to settle the contract, particularly where currency settlements are tightly controlled by local governments. Alternative methods of hedging will have to be used in these situations.

Forward rates are generally available up to a period of two years, this being a market definition of 'short' term. Between two and five years, or 'medium' term, there is growing depth, particularly in £/US$, US$DM and US$/Sfr markets. 'Long' term is a period in excess of five years. In these instances the bank would probably have to 'shop around' for a quote and a means to offload its risk. This is generally true of the majority of banks; however, certain very large banks are willing to take 'positions' on to their books and will therefore be able to quote a forward rate immediately for any date.

Quoted rates tend to be 'finer', i.e. the spread between the bid and offer narrower, when quoted for a straight date rather than a broken date. A straight date is, say, one, two or three months value date from the spot date. For example:

Spot value	1 December
Straight forwards – 1 month	1 January
– 2 months	1 February
and so forth	

A broken date would be a date falling in between the straights, such as 15 January or 2 February.

It is important to seek at least two quotes from various institutions for any currency sale/purchase, unless the amount involved is small. Banks will quote different rates dependent on their own currency 'position' or 'book'; i.e. whether they wish to buy or sell a currency may be influenced by their view and the risk they are already bearing in relation to that currency.

Application

Assumptions:

1. ABC Company is selling on 30-day net terms to Germany, and is invoicing in Deutschmarks. It expects to receive DM5,000,000 on the last day of each month from its customer.
2. The company firmly believes the Deutschmark will weaken against sterling, and decides to sell its receivables forward for the next three months. The rates quoted to sell Deutschmarks would be:

	£/DM
Spot value 31/1	2.7585
1 month forward premium	0.0152
1 month outright	2.7433
Spot value 31/1	2.7585
2 months forward premium	0.0332
2 months outright	2.7253
Spot value 31/1	2.7585
3 months forward premium	0.0459
3 months outright	2.7126

In the three instances the sterling amounts received would be £1,822,622, £1,834,660 and £1,843,250 respectively.

The advantage to ABC Company of selling forward is that it has crystallised its sterling receipt. The disadvantage occurs when, with hindsight, ABC's view on the direction of the DM/£ relationship is proved to be incorrect. For instance, the Deutschmark does not weaken but strengthens further, say to a spot rate at the end of each month of 2.7400, 2.7150 and 2.6978 respectively. In this instance ABC would have done better if it had not covered forward because it would have received, had it sold its receipts spot:

	£
1 month forward	1,824,817
2 months forward	1,841,620
3 months forward	1,853,362

The difference amounts to £19,267.

This monitoring and evaluation of decisions is an important part of the process. In ABC's case, the cost of this hedging decision might cause it to seek an alternative hedging technique in the future, or to decide that it will only hedge, say, 50% of its receivables – on the basis that it will not be wholly wrong.

A further disadvantage can arise if the anticipated receipt is not received with value on the maturity date of contract. ABC is still obliged to meet its full currency contract, and so in this instance would have to borrow the currency to meet the obligation and repay that borrowing when the currency is received. This can add to the overall cost of the transaction.

One further aspect to consider is that taxes may be levied on any gain/loss arising from a forward contract versus spot at maturity. This aspect will vary from country to country, and is not within the scope of this book.

Forward option contracts

These were developed as an extension to the foreign exchange contract to cater for situations when the date of the anticipated currency receipt is not specified. Therefore the forward exchange rate is fixed in the contract but not the settlement date. The company is, however, obliged to take up the contract between the start date of the option period and the end date. This differs from a currency option, which will be discussed later in this chapter.

There is some flexibility not only as to when the currency might be exchanged but also as to amount. In other words, the contract need not be settled all at once, but in tranches. If the total of the contract is not used it can be sold, at spot.

The availability of such options is similar to that of forward exchange contracts. The pricing is different, however, and more costly than the outright.

Application

Assumptions:

1. ABC Company is due to receive Sfr300,000 between 30 and 60 days hence.
2. The Swiss francs are to be sold for sterling.

3. ABC is seeking certainty in the transaction and wishes to sell the currency forward, rather than run the risk of waiting for spot.
4. The bank would make the following quote:

	£/Sfr
Spot value	2.3550
30 days premium	0.0152
Outright	2.3398
Spot value	2.3550
60 days premium	0.0297
Outright	2.3253

The most favourable rate for ABC to sell its Swiss francs is 2.3253. However, in order to compensate itself for the uncertainty as to when ABC will take up the forward contract, the bank will quote a rate to sell Swiss francs of 2.3398. It is this difference, in sterling terms, of £799 which is the cost to ABC of hedging the timing risk.

The advantage to ABC in using this type of contract is that receipts at unspecified dates can be covered, so no position is exposed. Where a company is receiving frequent small payments, which would be costly to cover individually, they may be parcelled together and covered under a global forward contract. As and when funds are received, an element of the contract can be exchanged.

The disadvantage is the cost.

Currency accounts

These may be set up to facilitate the hedging of currencies when used in conjunction with forward exchange contracts. Timing differences between actual dates of currency receipts/payments and those specified in the exchange contracts can be matched by drawing down or depositing the currency in a bank account. Not only will this method cater for any timing difference; it will also cater for differences in amount, so that round figures of currencies can be bought/sold rather than the exact amount. This is easier for the banks to handle and therefore less costly to the company.

The accounts will normally be held locally in the company's country, although this may be restricted either by local exchange controls or by those imposed by the country of the currency's origin. The availability is also dependent on credit lines being open to the company. The cost will be those relative to any account, while interest charges will reflect the applicable Euro rates. If the deposit amount is small, only a nominal deposit interest will accrue.

Application

Assumptions:

1. ABC Company is due to receive DM4,550,000 in 60 days' time.
2. It has taken out a forward exchange contract at a rate of 2.7253 and expects to sell the Deutschmarks then to receive £1,669,540
3. On the spot value date before maturity of the contract, i.e. two business days prior to day 60, ABC realises it will not receive the Deutschmarks as expected.
4. ABC instructs its bank to pay DM4,550,000 per the instructions under its contract, and to debit its current account accordingly.
5. The bank will act accordingly and charge ABC a Deutschmark interest rate on its borrowing, say, 4.5% p.a.
6. When ABC receives the Deutschmarks, it will credit its Deutschmark bank account, and so effectively repay the bank its loan.
7. As interest is denominated in Deutschmarks, ABC will have to purchase spot the amount necessary to cover interest due to the bank.
8. ABC will be able to cost out the effect of receiving the funds late.

		£
(a)	Original amount received under forward contract	1,669,540
(b)	DM interest cost of borrowing DM4,550,000 @ 4.5% for 1 week = DM3,981.25 bought at spot @ 2.7585	(1,443)
		1,668,097

As a result the effective forward rate achieved was DM4,550,000 ÷ £1,668,097 = 2.7276, versus the forward contract rate of 2.7253.

The converse would be true if the Deutschmark funds had been received early and were invested to earn interest between the receipt date and the forward contract maturity date.

As can be seen, the use of currency accounts affords greater flexibility in the handling of currency amounts. It saves the necessity and cost of entering into a new contract on actual receipt/payment date and effectively cancelling the original contract by entering into a separate equal and opposite transaction to mature on the original contract date. The disadvantages centre on the complexity of administering a number of currency accounts and keeping track of the overall exposure position.

Short-term deposit/borrowing combinations

A further hedging technique, in many ways an extension of the use of currency accounts, is to use the short-term money markets. If a company so chooses – due to high costs of cover, there being a wide interest rate differential in the forward rate, or where the timing of a transaction is unknown – it may borrow or deposit the currency now to create a hedge.

Like currency accounts the availability is subject to the use of credit lines and exchange control regulations. Costs of this method may be higher due to (a) more administration charges in accounting for the transaction; (b) costs of credit control; and (c) in the method itself since only in a perfect market will the interest differential between two currencies actually reflect the forward premium/discount. This is because the differential is calculated on deposit rates.

Application

Assumptions:

1. (a) ABC Company is selling a piece of land in France and is expecting to receive Ffr25,000,000 in about three months' time.
   (b) The company decides to hedge by borrowing the currency now and selling it for spot against sterling, investing the proceeds. The borrowing in French francs will be repaid from the receipt of funds.

Spot rate £/Ffr	9.3050	
3 month outright rate £/Ffr	9.2625	
3 month Ffr borrowing rate	9%	
3 month £ deposit rate	10.5%	

(i)	The company borrows Ffr25,000,000 for 3 months	
(ii)	The company sells for spot Ffr25,000,000 @ 9.3050	£2,686,727
(iii)	The company invests £2,686,727 for 3 months @ 10.5%	£69,560
(iv)	The company buys interest due on Ffr loan of Ffr562,500 @ 9.2625	£(60,728)
	'Profit'	£8,832
(v)	The Ffr25,000,000 is repaid from receipt of proceeds from sale of land	

A better method might be to borrow the French francs on a discounted basis, such that the principal plus interest on repayment totalled Ffr25,000,000.

2. Where ABC is aware it has to make a payment in currency at some point in the near future it could do the reverse and buy/borrow the currency now and invest the funds in order to meet the full commitment.
   (a) ABC Company is purchasing a small company in Switzerland. Completion is likely to occur in two months' time. The cost is Sfr11,675,000, comprising Sfr5,000,000 goodwill and Sfr6,675,000 net asset value.
   (b) ABC wishes to cover its risk exposure immediately. It has decided to cover the goodwill element by purchasing Swiss

francs, as this cost will be written off against reserves in its accounts. In managing its balance sheet exposure, matching foreign assets with liabilities, it has decided to borrow the balance on an ongoing basis.

(c) Today's rates are:

Spot rate £/Sfr	2.3350
2 month outright rate £/Sfr	2.3100
2 month borrowing rate Sfr	4% p.a.
2 month deposit rate Sfr	$3\frac{5}{8}$ p.a.

		£
(i)	ABC buys Sfr5,000,000	(2,141,327)
(ii)	ABC invests Sfr5,000,000 for 2 months @ $3\frac{5}{8}$% p.a. = Sfr30,208 @ 2.3100	13,077
(iii)	ABC borrows Sfr6,675,000	(2,858,672) (notional value @ 2.3350)
(iv)	ABC invests Sfr6,675,000 for 2 months @ $3\frac{5}{8}$% p.a. = Sfr40,328 @ 2.3100	17,458
(v)	Cost of borrowing Sfr6,675,000 for 2 months at 4% p.a. = Sfr44,500 @ 2.3100	(19,264)
	Cost of investment	(4,988,728)

ABC will use invested funds to meet the amounts due on completion of purchase of the company. The effective rate of this transaction hedged in this manner is:

$$\frac{11{,}675{,}000}{4{,}988{,}728} = 2.3403$$

This represents a 'profit' of £11,272 against the spot price of 2.3350, and £65,384 against a forward outright of 2.3100. If the spot rate on a completion date had strengthened above 2.3403, then ABC would have reduced its cost of the purchase by waiting. However, it had the certainty of knowing the cost of its investment earlier.

Futures contracts

The basic conceptual use of futures contracts and their terminology were explained in Chapter 7. To recap, however, a future is a legally binding contract to deliver or take delivery of a specified amount and quality of a financial instrument (commodity) on a given date, at an agreed price. The price is fixed now for an applicable future date.

Currency futures were first traded on the IMM (the International Monetary Market, a division of the Chicago Mercantile Exchange) in 1972. Contracts are now traded in Philadelphia, London, Singapore and Sydney.

The following example gives details of currency futures contracts:

Exchange Contract	IMM		LIFFE	
	£	DM	£	DM
Unit of trading	£25,000	DM125,000	£25,000	DM125,000
Delivery months	Jan, Mar, Apr, June, July, Sept, Oct, Dec, & spot month		Mar, June, Sept & Dec	
Price quotation	In US$ per unit of currency		In US$ per unit of currency	
Minimum price movement & value	0.05 cents per £1 ($12.50)	0.01 cents per DM1 ($12.50)	0.05 cents per £1 ($12.50)	0.01 cents per DM1 ($12.50)
Price limit	5 cents ($1,250)	1 cent ($1,250)	5 cents	1 cent
Trading hours	7.30 a.m.–1.24 p.m.	7.30 a.m.–1.20 p.m.	8.30 a.m.–3.00 p.m.	8.35 a.m.–3.00 p.m.
	(Chicago time)		(London time)	

There are standard contracts in most major currencies, including the yen and Swiss francs. In some local exchanges other currency contracts will exist, e.g. Canadian dollars in Montreal, Australian dollars in Sydney and, as an exception, the ECU in New York and Chicago.

A hedger using currency financial futures is seeking to transfer the risk of currency exposure by taking a position in the futures market equal and opposite to that which exists in the cash market. This assumes that the futures market will move in line with the underlying cash market.

Pricing

The fair price of a futures contract is determined using the concept of basis. This is defined as the difference between the price of the currency in the spot market and that in the futures market, i.e. the discount or premium reflecting differential at the forward date between the two currencies. For example:

Spot value £/US$: 1.5440
3 month Euro £ rate: 10.5%
3 month Euro $ rate: 7.5%
Interest differential: 3%

Using the formula:

$$\frac{\text{Spot rate} \times \text{time} \times \text{interest rate differential}}{100 \times \text{time}} = \frac{1.5440 \times 3 \times 3}{100 \times 12} = 0.0116$$

The pound is at a premium relative to the dollar; therefore the outright would be:

$$\begin{array}{r} 1.5440 \\ -0.0116 \\ \hline 1.5324 \end{array}$$

The premium of 116 pips is the 'basis', and the outright of 1.5324 is the theoretical futures price.

An alternative method of calculating the theoretical price is to establish the premium or discount using the futures market implied interest rates.

The difference between the theoretical price and the actual futures price is called the value basis. This measures how under- or overvalued the futures contract is relative to the cash market (the outright rate). If the two rates diverge widely then arbitrageurs would bring them back into line. In any case both basis (the difference between the spot exchange rate and the futures price) and value basis (the difference between the futures price and the equivalent outright rate) will be zero at the time of delivery. This is called convergence.

As indicated below, all four contracts are quoted against the US dollar, though in dollar terms – i.e. the dollars per unit of the currency concerned (save yen, where it is dollars per 100 yen). The quotes would therefore look like this:

£	Contract quoted as 1.5325	(US$/£)
DM	Contract quoted as 0.5506	(US$/DM)
Sfr	Contract quoted as 0.6510	(US$/Sfr)
Yen	Contract quoted as 0.6506	(US$/100 yen)

The exchange stipulates a minimum price movement and value. This minimum price interval is known as a 'tick'. In the sterling contract it is 5 cents. Accordingly, the next price level from 1.5325 could only be 1.5320 or 1.5330. In the Deutschmark contract this minimum level is 1 cent. The value of each tick is the same across all the contracts; for example:

£ Contract: 25,000 × 0.05 cents = US$12.50 per contract

DM Contract: 125,000 × 0.01 cents = US$12.50 per contract

Contracts are purchased by giving an order to a broker who can trade on the market floor. The trading itself is by the open outcry system. Settlement of the contract by the broker, acting on the client's behalf, is through an independent clearing-house, which is not a trader itself.

In London this is the International Commodities Clearing House (ICCH). The ICCH guarantees contracts to the clearing members; therefore the credit risk inherent in the contract is not with the other party. In return for the guarantee the ICCH requires margins to be paid on all contracts. These are held as security. There are two types of margin:

1. An initial margin is a deposit representing a percentage of the face value of the contract. The actual amount will vary depending on the contract terms. It is payable when a contract is entered into, and repaid on liquidation of the position.
2. A variation in maintenance margin can be payable daily since each contract is valued daily ('marked to the market'), and funds may be required to restore the initial margin level.

In practice the ICCH calls for margins from the clearing member, which in turn calls for funds from its clients. Should the customer be unable to cover the margin calls at any time, the clearing member is entitled to liquidate the position. In addition to the margin calls, the customer will have to pay commission costs to its broker (the clearing-house member). These are usually negotiable.

The futures market is not widely used for hedging currency exposure due to complexity and costs. In addition, the well-developed forward cash markets and more recently the currency option markets, which are in themselves more simple and effective, have further detracted from the use of the futures market by corporates.

Option contracts

The holder of an option contract has the right, but not the obligation, to buy or sell a specific amount of currency at a specific exchange rate on or before a specific date. Such a contract will be described as an American-style option. If the contract were exercisable only on its expiry date, it would be called a European-style option. The most commonly traded options are American-style because of their added flexibility.

Options are traded on exchanges such as LIFFE, Philadelphia or the Chicago Board of Options Exchange (CBOE), or they may be traded over the counter (OTC), direct with a bank.

The following example gives details of exchange contract specifications:

Exchange	Philadelphia (PHLX)	LIFFE
Contract	£	£
Unit of trading	£12,500	£25,000
Delivery months	March, June, September and December	
Price quotation	In US$ per unit of currency	
Minimum price movement & value	0.05c per £1 ($6.25)	0.01c per £1 ($2.50)
Price limit	5 cents	5 cents
Trading hours	8.30 a.m.–2.30 p.m. (Eastern time)	8.34 a.m.–4.02 p.m. (London time)

The range of currencies traded on the exchanges is similar to that of the futures market. However, the range is wider when dealing over the counter. If a bank runs a book in a currency, it will frequently offer options in that currency too. These OTC options are really bespoke since a bank will be flexible as to amounts and expiry dates. As a result, options traded on an OTC basis rather than through an exchange are more common.

There are specific terms referred to in the options markets. Those most frequently used are listed on page 178.

Pricing

There are five main determinants to the price of an option, or the premium: strike price, maturity, volatility, interest rate differential, and the market itself.

Strike price. The strike price is 'chosen' by the corporate. This may be at the money, in the money or out the money relative to today's spot forward rate.

In buying an option, the corporate is essentially taking out insurance cover to limit the downside potential of an open exposure position. The choice will therefore reflect this. It may be a budget rate or a marginal cost rate that is to be protected, or simply a rate in view of a possible market trend at which it would be beneficial to have a risk covered.

As is clear from the definitions of the three terms (see page 178), an at-the-money price is neutral to both holder and writer. An in-the-money price will be more favourable to the holder (the corporate) than the writer, and as such the premium will be higher than the at-the-money contract. The last situation, an out-the-money price, is immediately less attractive to the holder (the corporate) than the writer and the premium will therefore be less expensive than the at-the-money contract (see Fig. 8.1).

Maturity. Maturity will affect the cost of the option because the longer it is until the expiry date, the greater is the likelihood of volatility in

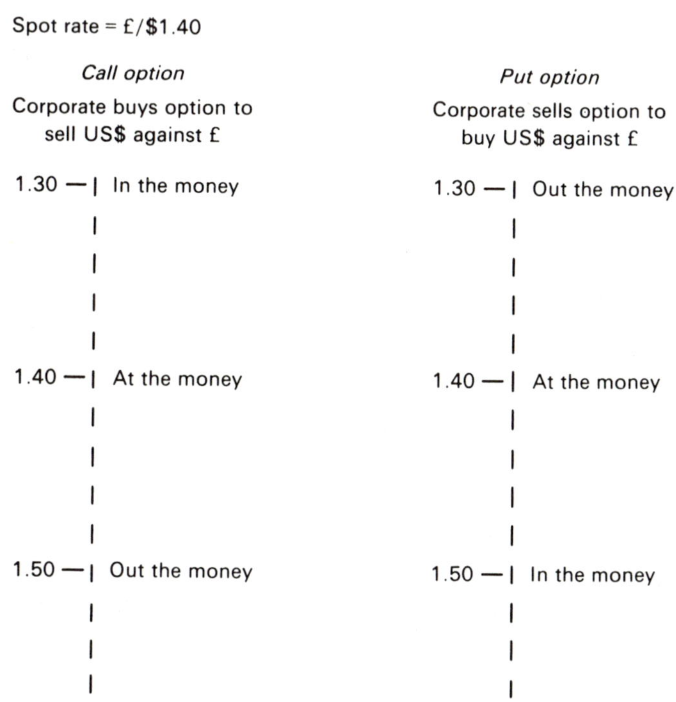

Fig. 8.1 Strike price.

the currency. This could therefore increase the probability that the holder (the corporate) will exercise the option. The writer (the bank) will compensate itself for this additional risk factor (see Fig. 8.2).

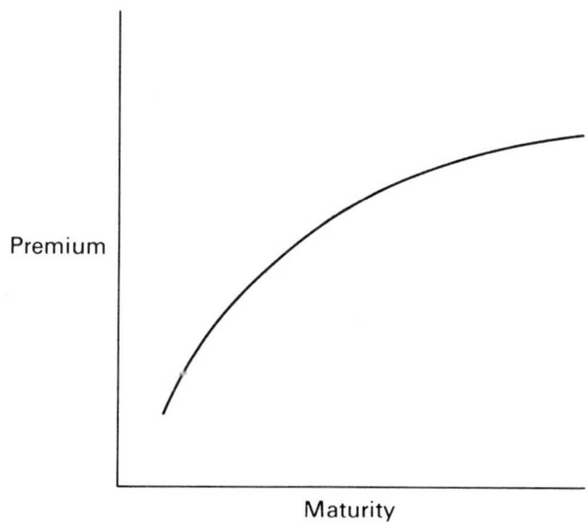

Fig. 8.2 Maturity.

Volatility. The volatility factor is the most difficult to assess in the pricing of an option. There have been many studies undertaken using statistical analysis to establish probabilities which can be used in a premium pricing model.

The most commonly used model is the Black–Scholes model, published in 1973, which was originally designed for the pricing of stock options. The model assumes that the exchange rate is a random variable in continuous time, which implies that over any particular time period the frequency distribution of the percentage change in the exchange rate has a normal distribution (see Fig. 8.3).

Percentage range above strike	Average value of range	Probability of occurrence*	Expected cost (premium)
Price	(A)	(B)	(A × B)
0–2	1		
2–4	3		
4–6	5		
↓	↓	↓	↓
		Total premium	

* This is based on a standard deviation calculation

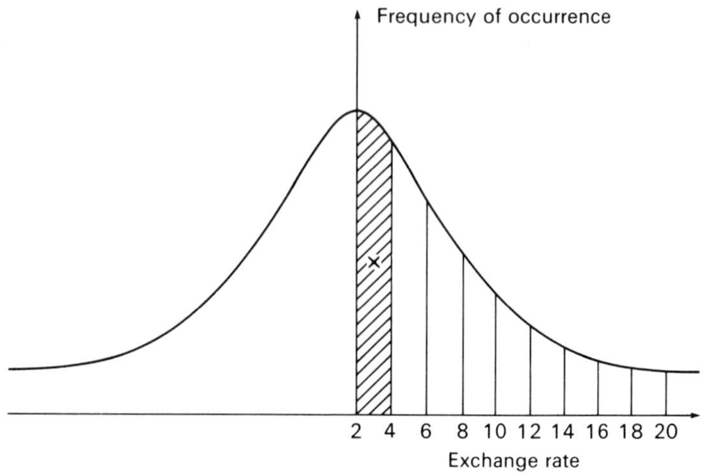

Fig. 8.3 Volatility.

In 1982 the Black–Scholes model was refined by Garman and Kohlhagen to cover currency options more specifically.

The curve is split into segments, each representing the probability of the exchange rate being – in this instance, 0–2%, 4–6%, etc. – higher than the original strike price. For example, if the shaded area X represents 10% of the total area of the curve, this implies the chance of the price being 0–2% above the strike price of maturity at 10%. If this is repeated for each segment a series of probabilities will arise. For each segment there is an average value to that range; i.e. for the 0–2% range, the average (straight line basis) is 1%, for the 2–4% range it is 3% (2 + 4 ÷ 2 = 3), and so forth (see table on page 113).

To calculate the premium the average range value is multiplied by the probability occurrence (the sum of the segment area calculation) for the whole curve, and then totalled.

Their formula is:

$$C(E) = \frac{[FN(d_1) - EN(d_2)]}{\begin{matrix} pt \\ e \end{matrix}}$$

Where:

$$d_1 = \left[\frac{\begin{matrix} \text{In } (F) & & (\sigma^2) & \\ (-) & + & (-) & t \\ (E) & & (2) & \end{matrix}}{\sigma\sqrt{t}} \right]$$

$$d_2 = d_1 - \sigma\sqrt{t}$$

F = forward exchange rate

E = exercise price

t = time to maturity

p = risk-free interest rate differential

σ = standard deviation of the continuously compounded annual rate of change of the exchange rate

$N(d)$ = the probability that a deviation less than d will occur in a normal distribution with a mean of zero and standard deviation of 1.

These models will be computerised by the option writers. It is consequently beyond the scope of this work to detail further.

The practitioner using options needs to be aware of how an option is priced rather than be able to do it. In the models the exchange rate volatility is measured in terms of frequency of percentage change, not the rate volatility itself. This is usually measured by reference to historical rates, with a weighting factor biased towards the most recent rates. However, the choice remains as to time-scale, and whether to use the daily opening or closing rates, the high or the low for the day, and so forth.

To summarise, the volatility element in an option price is the most crucial, and is based on the probability of an option being in the money at the expiry date and thus exercised by the holder of that option against the writer of that option.

Interest rate differentials. The interest rate differentials between the two currencies in an option are expressed in the cash market as a forward premium or a discount. The 'depth' of the premium or discount will affect the cost of carrying that option by a bank. This in turn may increase the premium to the holder.

Where a call option is purchased, the bank's cost of carry will be higher if there is a premium in the forward market (see Fig. 8.4).

In this instance the initial cost of the carry is 4.12% p.a., which will be factored into the premium price. If the forward rate were at a discount, say at 1.4800, there would be a negative cost of carry to the bank since the interest rate of the currency being bought is higher than that being sold.

The reverse is true where a put option (the right to sell a currency) is bought (see Fig. 8.5).

In this instance it costs the bank 2.83%, which is the interest forgone over three months by selling forward rather than spot. As

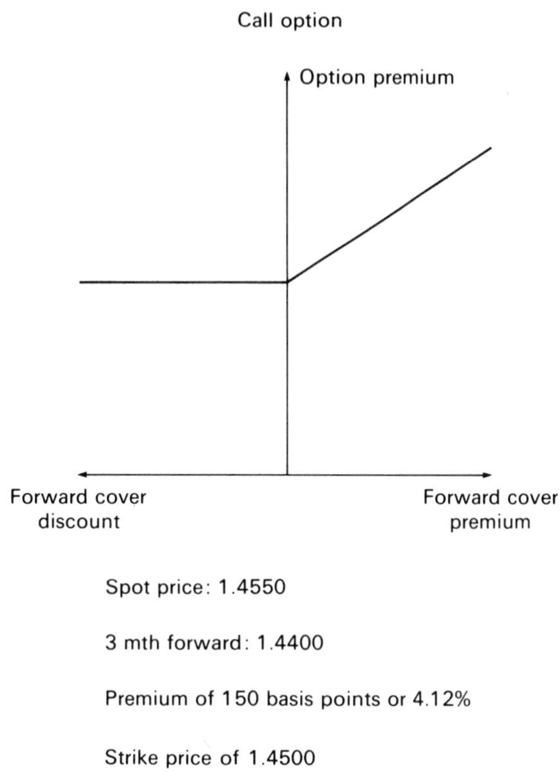

Fig. 8.4 Call option with premium.

before, if the currency were at a premium there would be a negative cost of carry to the bank.

The market. The market itself can affect options pricing. This is measured in the delta factor, which is the proportional amount the currency option premium will change for a given price change in the underlying currency. This is important when the market is illiquid in either the spot or forward dates, or is volatile with large swings. An option with a low delta value is less risky than one with a high delta.

Any instances which in essence will result in additional risk to the bank, and conversely value to the corporate, will be reflected in a higher option premium.

Uses

Options are a flexible tool in currency exposure management. They can be

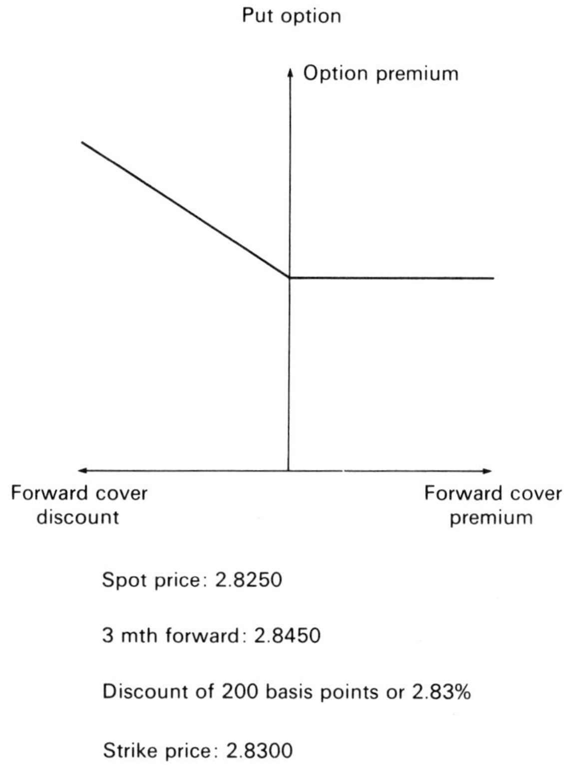

Fig. 8.5 Put option with discount.

used for covering import or export currency flows or, as is most common, tender periods on foreign contracts. In essence, options provide insurance to the holder against an adverse exchange rate move. The premium payable up front is a one-off cost, and can therefore be likened to an insurance premium.

There are two views regarding the evaluation of the premium. The first is that it is a sunk cost and therefore 'ignored'. The second is that it is an integral part of the hedging decision and should be evaluated, which may lead to a decision not to enter into an option. The choice can be predicated by circumstances, e.g. the scale and nature of the risk to be hedged.

The premium can be represented diagrammatically:

(a) The 'sunk' cost view – the strike price is the break-even rate (Fig. 8.6).
(b) Evaluation – the break-even rate is lower than the strike price (Fig. 8.7).

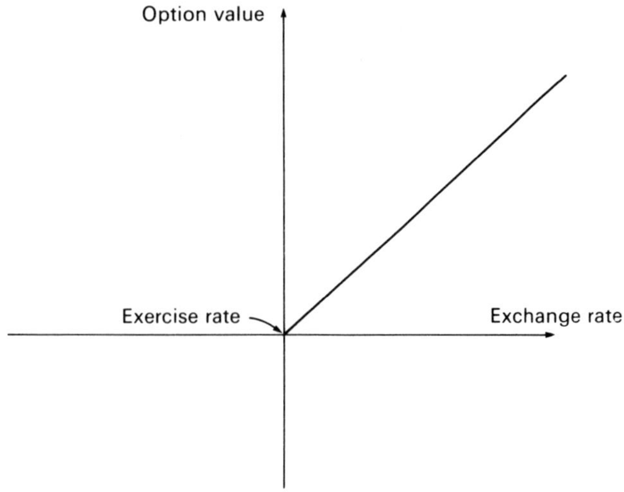

Fig. 8.6 Options premiums: the 'sunk' cost view.

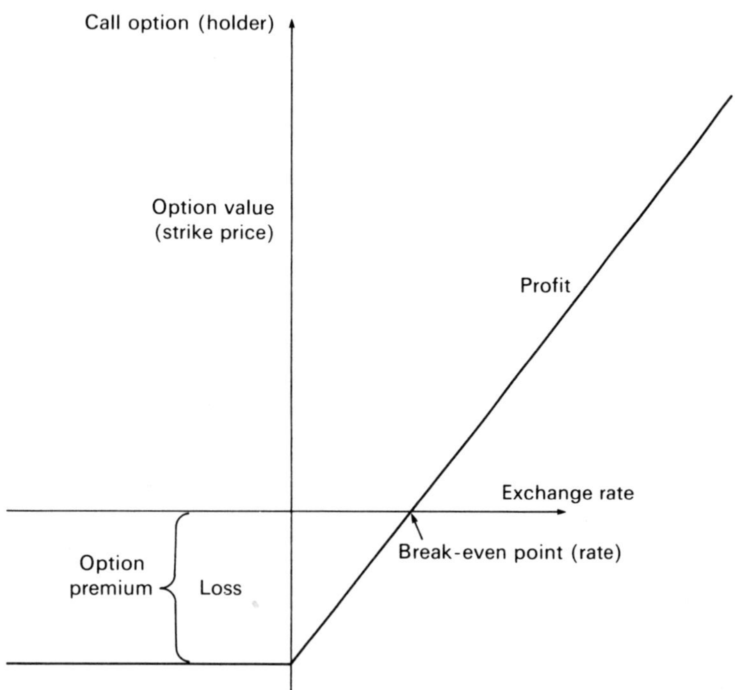

Fig. 8.7 Call option premium: evaluation.

In monetary terms, taking the following example on an option to buy £1 million and sell US dollars, three months forward:

Spot price	Strike price	Option premium (%)	Actual cost (£)
1.3800	1.40	1.67	16,700
Fwd 1.3900	1.45	0.66	6,600
	1.50	0.33	3,300

The option premium is a given figure:

(a) To calculate cost of option:

$$\frac{£1{,}000{,}000 \times 1.67}{100} = £16{,}700$$

(b) To evaluate break even rate, representing actual cost of selling equivalent US dollars on an all-in basis.

$$\frac{\text{Amount}}{\text{Strike price}} = \frac{1{,}000{,}000}{1.40} = \$714{,}285$$

$$\frac{\text{Amount + premium}}{\text{Proceeds at strike price}} = \text{Break-even rate}$$

$$\frac{£1{,}016{,}700}{\$714{,}285} = 1.4234$$

This means it is more costly by 234 pips to sell US dollars.

(c) As a check back to the option premium in percentage terms:

$$\frac{\text{Points difference in break-even rate}}{\text{Strike price}} = \frac{0.0234}{1.40} \times 100 = 1.67\%$$

The evaluation of whether it is still advisable to cover the exposure risk using this method will depend on the time-scale of the option, its size and, most importantly, the corporate's perception of future interest rates.

If the feeling is that the pound will strengthen (in the scenario of a call option where the holder has the right to buy currency, in this instance sterling) by 1.67% or more over the time horizon, then the corporate will enter into the option to lock in the downside risk. If this is thought unlikely then an alternative method of hedging may be chosen, or a lower strike price, further out the money, in order to reduce the premium charge.

In the instance of a put option where the holder is selling £1,000,000 to buy US dollars, the evaluation analysis is similar.

Spot price	Strike price	Option premium (%)	Actual cost (£)
1.3800	1.40	2.68	26,800
Fwd 1.3900	1.35	0.87	8,700
	1.30	0.36	3,600

(a) Cost of option:

$$\frac{£1{,}000{,}000 \times 2.68}{100} = £26{,}800$$

(b) To evaluate break-even:

$$\frac{1{,}000{,}000}{1.40} = \$714{,}285$$

$$\frac{£1{,}026{,}800}{\$714{,}285} = 1.4375$$

(c) To check premium:

$$\frac{0.0375}{1.40} \times 100 = 2.68\%$$

In this evaluation the corporate has an unlimited profit potential if sterling weakens, the option serving its purpose as the downside limit (Fig. 8.8).

For example, a UK company is due to receive US$1,000,000 in three months' time in settlement of sales of goods. The current spot price is 1.5000 and three months forward is 1.5000. There has been increased

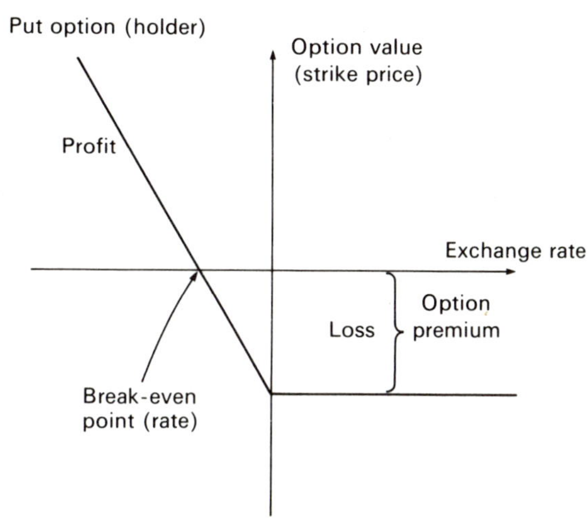

Fig. 8.8 Put option premium: evaluation.

volatility in the market and the company believes the US dollar will appreciate against sterling over the next three months – but wishes to protect itself should the dollar depreciate. The company would therefore contact its banker or broker (to trade on an exchange) to buy a three-month call option (option to buy foreign currency, in this instance sterling) at a strike price of 1.50. The cost is, say, 1.93% or 290 pips. This is equivalent to a break-even rate of 1.5290, i.e. more costly in selling dollars.

An option contract has a value through its life, based on the time it has left until maturity and the strike price versus the current spot rate. At expiry the option has no time value, but it may have a value against spot. For instance, if in the above example the spot rate at expiry is 1.60, the company would exercise its option to receive £666,667, i.e. US$1,000,000 @ 1.50. This contrasts with receiving in the market £625,000 @ 1.60 had the option not been entered into. However, if the spot rate at expiry is 1.40 then the option would not be exercised, as the company would choose to settle its receivable spot in the market. It would receive £714,286 versus the £666,667 it would have received under the contract.

Early exercise

If the option is American-style, it may be exercised prior to maturity. Unless a company is actively trading options, it will depend on the state of the underlying transaction.

For instance, if US$1,000,000 were received one month into the life of a three-month contract, that option may be worth more if sold than if exercised. This is because the contract itself has a time and intrinsic value.

Taking the earlier example, say US$1,000,000 was received after one month, when the new spot rate was 1.53. There are two possibilities:

(a) Exercise the option because the strike price is below the spot rate:

Description	£
US$1,000,000 @ 1.50	666,667
Cost of premium (£666,667 × 1.93%)	(12,867)
Total received	653,800
Without option would have received US$1,000,000 @ 1.53	(653,595)
Net benefit to the company	205

(b) Sell the option because of the value it has, because spot rate is 1.53 versus option strike price of 1.50. This value could be, say, 376 pips or 2.45% at 1.53, versus the original 290 pips, giving a net value of 86 pips, or 0.56% at 1.53.

Description	£
From sale of option (£666,667 × 2.45%)	16,333
Cost of premium	(12,867)
From sale of US$1,000,000 @ 1.53	653,595
Total received	657,061
Without option would have received US$1,000,000 @ 1.53	(653,595)
Net benefit to the company	3,466

Exchange-traded or over-the-counter options
The company may choose whether to purchase options through a recognised exchange, such as LIFFE, CBOE or Philadelphia, or to deal direct with its bankers. The differences may be summarised thus:

	Exchange	Over-the-counter
Contract terms	Standardised	Determined each transaction
Expiration	Standardised	Determined each transaction
Transaction method	Open outcry	Bank to client
Participants	Exchange members (brokers)	Banks
Commissions	Negotiable with broker	Negotiable – usually built into premium

On page 123 there is a summary of forwards, futures and options.

Range forward

A range forward is a foreign currency forward exchange contract that specifies a range of exchange rates within which the currencies may be exchanged at contract expiration. The corporate will specify the risk that is to be covered by choosing the upper or lower range limit. By mathematical formula, based on a volatility model, the bank will calculate the other limit to the range.

If at the date of maturity the actual exchange rate is outside the range, the effective rate will be the range limit as appropriate, If the actual exchange rate is within the range, the contract will not be exercised and the company will take spot. For example:

Range	US$/DM 1.8150–1.8500	
Actual exchange rates on maturity	(a)	US$/DM 1.8000
	(b)	US$/DM 1.8175
	(c)	US$/DM 1.8650

At maturity in situation (a) the effective rate would be 1.8150; in (b) 1.8175 the spot rate as it is within the range; and in (c) 1.8500 as 1.8650 is outside the range.

	Forwards	Futures	Options
Contract	Contractual obligation for buyer and seller	Contractual obligation for buyer and seller	Buyer of a call (put) has the right to take (make) delivery; seller has contractual obligation to potentially make (take) delivery
Size of contract	Determined	Standardised	Standardised on an exchange, determined each transaction OTC
Delivery date	Determined in transaction	Standardised	Standardised on an exchange, determined each transaction OTC; also, if American-style, option can be exercised at any time before expiration
Delivered instrument	Full value of contract	Full value of contract at final settlement price	Full value of contract
Method of transaction	Direct contact between buyer and seller	Open auction on registered exchange	Open auction on registered exchange or direct OTC
Issuer and guarantor	No third party, principal to principal	Exchange, clearing house	Exchange, clearing-house or principal to principal OTC
Costs	No margin necessary	Initial and variation margin, daily variation	Premium costs, fixed, payable at start of contract

CHAPTER 9

Control systems

CHAPTER AIM

To identify areas of cash management requiring control; to detail internal and external control measures and checks; to look at insurance aspects.

INTERNAL CONTROL

Control over a department such as cash management is essential. It should be detailed, documented and rigorously complied with, and as a minimum two people should be involved in the decision/action process.

The chief concern is in relation to the movement of money out of the company's accounts – particularly where funds are transferred on the back of telephone or telex instructions to third parties. In this respect the introduction of electronic funds transfer methods can alleviate some concerns.

Control is also required over position reporting. There should be an automatic reporting system so that no items can be omitted, and it should be checked and reviewed by senior management. This would include any treasury computer systems. Another aspect of reporting is the recording of all transactions in a diary (manually or on the computer) for reference daily.

The employee selection procedure needs careful control. References must be taken up and an initial period of employment must be agreed to prior to allowing the new employee powers to commit the company's funds.

All control measures should be collated into a departmental procedures manual as they are agreed or changed. The manual will outline the objectives of the department; the guidelines or parameters within which it must operate; its activities, including how transactions are to be effected; and any specific items such as the interface with subsidiaries where the department acts on their behalf. The contents of the manual will have been agreed with senior management. It will then provide a reference for audit checks.

Control rests heavily on the concept that at least two people are involved in any decision or authorisation process. Collusion is of course a danger, but if a third element is introduced, say another department monitoring bank balances, the risks will be reduced.

All transactions must be approved, ideally on preprinted standard forms. Approval dockets may be separate or integral to the document recording the transaction.

The preprinted forms recording transactions should be 'working' forms too. At a later date it is often helpful to review which other banks were asked to quote, and what their relative performance was. Figures 9.1 to 9.6 provide examples of approval forms and record slips.

These forms can be in multipart since other departments will need the information too.

The following items should be noted on the forms:

1. Serial numbers. On the dealing and currency dealing tickets, the transfer slips have the identical serial numbers too in order to facilitate the audit trail.
2. A comments section, detailing the reason for the transaction.
3. Notice dates or action dates. In currency-related transactions, notice date is always two business days prior to the value or maturity date. All transactions should be diarised by *action* date, not maturity date.
4. The originator of the deal, the checker (the person who checked the calculations involved) and the authoriser.

Part of the control process is to ensure all three boxes have been initialled by at least two persons to indicate compliance.

Authority levels must be delegated to avoid inefficiencies. The levels will be relative to the size of the transaction normally undertaken by a department.

Three distinct types of authority can be distinguished.

Signatory powers

Wherever possible, there should be at least two signatories to each bank account and financial transaction. These may be from a selection of authorised signatories who will have been approved at board level prior to informing the banks, and who will be minuted as such.

LOAN/DEPOSIT/DRAWDOWN
Approval

Company:

Docket no. ....
Date ....

Bank:

Currency:		Value date:
Amount:		
Interest due/receivable:		

Indicative rates: Time:

	Screen (LIBID/LIBOR)	Bank (Margin incl/excl)
1 week		
1 month		
2 months		
3 months		
6 months		
9 months		
12 months		

Comments (inc. original reason for borrowing):

Recommendation:

Interest	Purchase required (see attached)	To be paid ex	Accrue	Transfer

Originator:

Interest ....
Period agreed ....
Approved by ....
Date ....

Fig. 9.1 Loan/deposit/drawdown approval.

PURCHASE/SALE
Approval

Docket no. ....

Date ....

Company:

Currency:		VS
Amount:		
Value date:		

Indicative rates: Time:

Screen Bank

Spot

1 month ....

2 months ....

3 months ....

6 months ....

9 months ....

12 months ....

Purpose:

Funds to be paid to/from

Originator:

Yes/No

Approved by ....

Date ....

Fig. 9.2 Purchase/sale approval.

DEALING RECORD SLIP

Docket no. ....
Company: Date ....
Lender/borrower: Time ....
Broker: Auth. ....

Currency amount	Deposited		Notice Date
	Drawndown		
	Rollover		
	Repay		

Ext.				
Bank				
Contact				
Tel.				
Rates				

Value date		Days 360/365	Rate:	Interest due:
From:	To:			

Delivery instructions

Given:	Received:

Comments:

Maturing interest paid:	Yes/No/N.A.	Amount:
accrued:	Yes/No/N.A.	Total due:
Confirmation sent:	Yes/No	Telex/Letter
received:	Yes/No	Telex/Letter
Diarised:	Yes/No	
Originator:		
Checker:		
Master diary:	Yes/No	

Fig. 9.3 Dealing record slip.

CURRENCY DEALING SLIP

Docket no. ....

Company: — Date ....

Transaction title: — Time ....

Auth. ....

Currency sold			Value date
Currency purchased			

Deal rate	Notice date:	
	Target rate:	Screen rate:

Ext:				
Banks:				
Contact:				
Telephone:				
Rates:				

Delivery instructions:

Given:	Received:

Confirmation sent:	Yes/No	Telex/Letter
received:	Yes/No	Telex/Letter
Diarised:	Yes/No	
Originator:		
Checker:		
Master diary:	Yes/No	

Fig. 9.4 Currency dealing slip.

RECEIPT TRANSFER RECORD SLIP

Company

Docket no. ....

Date ....

Receipts

Currency	Amounts	Value dates

Fund movements

From:	To:

Comments:	Screen rate:
	Rate given

Confirmation sent:	Yes/No	Telex/Letter		
received:	Yes/No	Telex/Letter		
Diary:	Yes/No	Master diary	Yes/No	

Originator .... Actioned by ....

Checker .... Time ....

Fig. 9.5 Receipt transfer record slip.

PAYMENT TRANSFER RECORD SLIP

Company

Docket no. ....

Date ....

Currency	Amounts	Value dates

Fund movements

From:	To:

Comments:	Screen rate:
	Rate given:

Confirmation sent: Yes/No Telex/Letter

received: Yes/No Telex/Letter

Diary Yes/No Master diary Yes/No

Originator .... Actioned by ....

Authorised by .... Time ....

Fig. 9.6 Payment transfer record slip.

Signing powers will likely reflect seniority. If a signatory leaves a company, the company's bankers should be informed of when his signatory powers cease. Signatory powers may be further differentiated between transactions involving the commitment of the company's funds, i.e. payments of any sort, and receipts into the company's accounts. The latter may or may not be confirmed by the company to the bank. If there are, the company may not require these to be 'authorised'.

'Voice' powers

These will be the personnel within cash management, and immediate superiors, who are authorised to issue instructions over the telephone regarding the dealing in or movement of the money. This list should be updated if there are personnel changes, and it may differentiate between those able to deal and those only able to transfer funds to and from the company's accounts.

Commitment powers

These refer to entering into new facilities with banks and institutions, giving company guarantees or letters of comfort, and so forth. These powers will be delegated from the board to certain levels of senior management.

The interaction of these three levels would typically be as follows. A new facility is set up with a bank under the board's delegated powers to commit the company. Subsequently deals and transactions are effected by the authorised 'voices', which are then confirmed in writing by the company to its bankers. The letter will be signed by two authorised signatories.

The board will also be asked to approve two sets of limits.

Dealer limits

These will detail the guidelines for dealers regarding the amount of funds they may borrow or deposit in any one transaction, the range of banks or institutions they may contact, whether they can undertake any trading in currencies for profit or arbitrage between instruments for profit, and so forth. The guidelines would be issued to each dealer, and strict compliance monitored. The result of non-compliance should be made clear to the dealer.

Deposit limits

These refer to the maximum amount of money or currency equivalent that can be deposited with an institution, bank or otherwise, at any one time. The limits will be reviewed from time to time, but at least annually. Again, the result of non-compliance should be clarified.

Internal control and checking procedures are the first stage, and should be reinforced by audit checks from time to time. In many aspects the internal check will interface with the external one.

EXTERNAL CONTROL

Bank mandates

Banks, in setting up accounts, require bank mandate forms to be filled in. These specify how the account will be operated, and will detail the following:

1. How many signatories are required to authorise a cheque, specimens of the authorised signatories, and any limits attached.
2. How telephone transfers will be actioned, by whom, and who may then confirm in writing. A list of authorised signatories will be provided if different from (1) above.
3. To whom confirmations of transactions should be sent. This should be to an accounting department, separate from cash management.
4. Any other specific items, such as maximum size of debits.

Electronic funds transfer

Electronic funds transfer (EFT) is more widely used now. In deciding which system to use, a key feature is security. Internal audit should be involved to ensure that the process of check and control is strictly adhered to.

These systems hinge on the use of passwords; therefore no one person should know the full range of passwords. Typically the senior passwords, allowing the release of money, will be known only to already authorised signatories in order to maintain the control measures. However, because confirmatory letters are not required under these systems and only one signatory would input the release password, there is a greater burden on the signatory to check the transaction details.

There has been much discussion as to which is more 'secure', EFT or telephone transfers subsequently confirmed in writing. Errors can arise in the input of EFT instructions, just as misreading instructions can occur when telephoning the bank. However, in the former case there is another checker before funds are released. Secondly, with telephone transfers it is likely the funds will have been 'moved' prior to the bank receiving the written confirmation of instructions. In order to cope with these problems, many companies send telex confirmations on a tested or untested basis immediately after the transaction has been agreed. This ensures that any discrepancies can be sorted out before funds are 'moved'. The 'fear' regarding EFT is a threat of hackers illegally entering the system and diverting funds.

As part of the general control process, external auditors should be encouraged to do an audit check on the procedures and systems.

INSURANCE

Companies can take out employee fidelity guarantee insurance to cover themselves against employee fraud. To do this the company would discuss in detail, and specify in the policy, the procedures of check and control as outlined above.

CHAPTER 10

Performance measurement

CHAPTER AIM

To assess the department's resource requirements; to endeavour to quantify performance measures.

The resource requirements of a cash management department will vary depending on the department's role within the organisation. If the organisation is highly decentralised so that the department plays a monitoring and control role, the resources would revolve around an efficient communications system. Alternatively, if highly centralised the department would need people capable of dealing effectively in the market, with good computer back-up.

RESOURCES

People

The cash management area within a treasury function can be highly specialised, requiring high-calibre people. They will need to possess attributes such as excellent attention to detail; a sense of responsibility, the ability to work in a team; good telephone and interpersonal skills; the ability to work efficiently under stress; and the capacity for a good interpretation of financial markets and the company's role within them. This is not an exhaustive list, and each company will require its own set of skills. The above attributes will apply to all members of the team, including back-up staff.

Information services

As already noted, information is vital. The cash management department will therefore need access to real time services and database services (see Chapter 3). Ideally, each dealer should have his own screen to access information relative to the position he is monitoring.

The department will require computer-based back-up. This may be in the form of database storage but is more likely to be an interactive system.

The concept of the treasury work station will allow the user to model, analysing 'what if' situations before dealing; to provide pre-deal support; to process the transaction details and produce confirmations; and to produce management reports on the company's outstanding positions.

Each of these functions is important in the overall running of exposures. Modelling capabilities allow more alternatives to be considered; if not done by computer they would be too time-consuming to work through, particularly in volatile markets. Pre-deal support is a control feature, allowing the dealer to check the company's outstandings with the banks being approached. The report formats will allow the company's positions to be 'marked to market' so that exposures can be revalued. They also provide a means of informing senior management about transactions undertaken and positions held.

Information from external sources can be fed direct into the work station – e.g. bank balances and figures from other departments or subsidiaries all reported electronically.

Communication services

These are based on the telephone, telex, telefax and direct computer links. The company may have direct lines put into the dealing room. These save outsiders and dealers having to wait for connections through the company's switchboard. Alternatively, direct lines into the banks or brokers may be installed. When the corporate dealer pushes the switch to connect to a bank, for example, the company's name lights up on the bank dealer's board and the contact is made.

Due to the volume of telex information exchanged between the department, its fellow subsidiaries and the banks, a direct link into the company's telex system, or its own system, can prove cost-effective.

COST/PROFIT CENTRE

Setting up a corporate dealing room can be costly, as it will include specialised people, computerisation, and special furniture to accommodate screens, people, telex, air conditioning, telephones and so on. As with any other area, the company will naturally expect a return on this investment – which will occur where costs have been minimised and returns maximised. This process of evaluation should be automatic (see below), whether or not the department is designated a profit centre in its own right.

In most companies the treasury/cash management function is regarded as a service area for the rest of the group. This would conflict in part with designating it a profit centre as well. However, the function of the department can be split between the two so that motivation is provided to individuals. The key in monitoring this is the process of evaluating any agreed performance measures.

Performance measures

These fall into two categories according to whether or not they can be specified in money terms.

Float management

The object is to minimise float time when receiving money and to maximise when paying it out (see Chapter 6). There are ways of reducing/increasing float times which are quantifiable in money terms. Any float system needs monitoring to ensure efficiencies are maintained.

The first stage is to monitor the timeliness of debit and credit clearing in the original system. In order to be meaningful, this survey must take into account the bulk of the regular debit and credit flows. There will be items, such as overseas payments and receipts, which take longer to clear and these should be reviewed separately. A review could be made on the basis of base currency items within the country, base currency items abroad, and foreign currency items, each type being split between receipts and payments.

When the review is complete, the company can look at ways of improving the float time, in particular credit clearing. Where payment methods are improved, in particular by foreign suppliers, it may be possible to negotiate a reduction in price.

Improvements may be effected if the company moves to a bank with a wider branch network, which complements its geographical spread. This will prove more efficient when netting sums within the group, and will be costly in charges. The method of paying by cheque may be improved by local presenting of cheques, or, where there are items of a sufficient size, by arranging special collection for them. Improved collection methods may be used, such as having a lockbox in the USA or

Canada, or opening an account in the branch where the largest customer banks.

Payments may be made by telegraphic transfer, or electronically, to replace the cheque, or bills of exchange may be used abroad, as payment to the supplier will be guaranteed on the due date, if that bill has been accepted and confirmed by a bank.

If a change is contemplated, the benefit or otherwise can be costed to compare with the original system. For instance:

Overdraft balance	(1,036,444) (cleared balance)
One-day float	190,546
Two-day float	567,034
Overdraft rate	10.5%

The amounts held in 'float' are those items that will go into the company's account in one or two days. As these items are positive, the overdraft will be reduced. The bank calculates overdraft interest on the daily cleared balance. Therefore, on a balance of 1,036,444, interest for one day would be 298. If the clearing was improved by one day, the balance on day one would be 845,898, being 1,036,444 minus 190,546. The interest would have been 243, a saving of 55.

Bank charges

Banks charge for the services they provide, and therefore these need controlling. This control may be on absolute levels, a per item basis or volume basis.

A company needs to assess the most appropriate method of charging to suit its method of operation. For a cash-retailing business, such as a supermarket, there will be a high volume of low value cheques, notes and coin. In this instance it would be cheaper for the company to seek a turnover (volume) charge, as a per item charge, particularly on low value cheques, might be disproportionately high. Alternatively, if a company is in heavy manufacturing, or is in a professional service type industry, the likelihood is that the number of cheques will be less, but the value greater. In this instance the companies would seek a per item charge basis as a flat cost. Again, the instances can be costed by taking a sample and comparing the cost on different charging bases.

Interest charges/revenues

The formula for monitoring the equivalent cost of borrowing was introduced in Chapter 7; it can be used as a target against which performance is evaluated. The same is true for the investment of surplus funds where the target rate is set. In both instances they are money items on which an evaluation can be made.

This area is perhaps the 'easiest' to monitor under performance criteria. Once a target has been defined and agreed, it is a case of calculating actual versus 'base'.

It is important when setting the target that it is not automatic, otherwise there is no incentive to do better. An automatic target would be, say, base rate or prime rate.

In reporting actual versus target a simple format can be devised. For instance:

A	B	C	D	E	F	G
Amount	Days outstanding	Target rate	Interest cost $\frac{A \times B \times C}{365 \quad 100}$	Actual rate	Interest cost $\frac{A \times B \times E}{365 \quad 100}$	Benefit/ (cost) (D−F)
5,000,000	1	9.75	1335.62	9.50	1301.37	34.25

This format can be used whether the target refers to a deposit (investment) rate or borrowing rate.

The cash management department would be monitored on the basis of column G. If the target is consistently 'beaten', then it may require reviewing. It should also be realised that, if the borrowing or deposit is for a term period such as three or six months, then the target rate should be consistent. For easy monitoring, it would be prudent to have only two rates, one for the short term, up to three months, and one for medium term, three to 12 months. These periods would be chosen in line with the company's strategy. The rates themselves would be a weighted average of an amalgam of market quoted rates. For instance base rate, plus seven days' notice rate, plus three months' LIBOR, or base rate plus three months' LIBOR, plus nine months' LIBOR. The opportunities are varied.

Currency hedging

The setting of a target to evaluate the benefit or otherwise of a hedging strategy is subjective. There are three possibilities, regardless of the method of hedging chosen:

1. The spot rate on maturity.
2. The forward rate when the decision was made.
3. The best rate available between the two dates.

Each has an effect regarding the motivation of the department. Although the measure is in money terms, it is subjective because the measurement criteria are inexact.

The 'easiest' method of measurement, and that probably most widely used, is the reference rate of spot rate on maturity. It is readily ascertainable, either from a local bank or the financial press. Even this is a rough measure as the exchange rate moves during the day, but a consistent rate should be used, such as the opening or closing rate as quoted by a reference bank.

The format for reporting is similar to that for interest/revenue recording. For instance:

A	*B*	*C*	*D*	*E*	*F*
Currency amount (B = Bought) (S = Sold)	Original rate	Base currency amount (A−B) or (A×B)	Rate on maturity	Revised base currency amount (A−D) or (A×D)	Exchange difference (C−E)
US$500,000(S)	1.4850	£336,700	1.6555	£302,024	£34,676
FFR 100.000(B)	9.7860	£10,219	9.9715	£10,029	£(190)

Risk management

A company has many financial risks to contemplate. A crude analysis can be made on actions taken versus those not taken. However, when taking action to reduce risk, further action stages are sometimes required. This will mitigate against straight comparisons, though some attempt should be made.

Risk management is usually associated with the corporate finance assessment of a company, and capital market issues, which are outside the scope of this book. However, some analysis can be undertaken, when the options and risk management are being reviewed, as to the balance sheet and earnings per share effect. The factors tend to be reviewed at senior management level and as such are not included in the performance measurement of the cash management department.

Performance measurement is difficult to assess in the treasury function owing to the variety of ways that risks can be managed, and the volatility of the markets, which will affect the decision as to the timing of transactions. However, some attempts should be made but whichever performance criteria are chosen as methods of evaluating the department, they should be detailed, agreed and documented. This is particularly important if they are to be used in the process of judging the remuneration of personnel.

CHAPTER 11

Summary

The theme of this book has been to try to set the role of cash management in the context of the company. It is important to recognise how differing companies will require their respective cash departments to be sourced individually.

This is obviously the first stage in setting up a department. The second is to ensure that communications – particularly in terms of information flow – are efficient, both into and out of the function.

The prime role of the cash management area is to manage effectively and efficiently the flow of funds through the company. To do this it will identify exposure risks, of whatever type; it will make recommendations and take action on these risks, seeking the best option to manage the risk; and it will monitor the performance of decisions and actions taken.

A key area where an active cash department is being managed is that of considering changes, and whether these should impact on risk exposures already covered. This involves looking at 'what if' situations.

Whenever a cash management function is set up by a company – whether it is to be centralised or decentralised in its attitude to servicing the company's money requirements, and whether it is to be active in the markets or not – clear departmental guidelines should be laid down and control parameters set.

Appendix: Banking systems

The aim of this Appendix is to appreciate the key aspects of clearing and wholesale banking systems, and the exchange controls of the world's major trading countries.

Major countries chosen revolve around the Group of Ten, a phrase coined in the early 1980s to refer to a group of countries whose finance ministers periodically meet to discuss world financial matters. The Group comprises the United Kingdom, the United States, Canada, Japan, Germany, France, the Netherlands, Belgium, Italy and Sweden. The details of the Swiss and Australian banking systems are also reviewed here.

UNITED KINGDOM

Central bank, regulatory and monetary control

The central bank of the United Kingdom is the Bank of England. It regulates the banks, and acts as banker to the government and private-sector banks. It has responsibility for the day-to-day supervision and control of the foreign exchange and money markets.

Banks are defined under the terms of the Banking Act 1979. This specifies that if an institution wishes to carry on a deposit-taking business it is required to seek recognition from the Bank of England as either a recognised bank or a licensed deposit-taker. The criteria laid down in the Act distinguish the two types of institution. Basically the distinction rests on the range of services provided and the bank's reputation and standing in the financial community, although only a recognised bank may describe itself as a 'bank'.

The Act also introduced the term 'representative office', referring to a representative of an overseas deposit-taking institution establishing an office in London. The institution is required to inform the Bank of England. It cannot however take deposits without having first gained recognised banking or licensed deposit-taking status.

The Banking Act 1987 abolished the distinction between recognised banks and licensed deposit-takers and instituted a single regime to cover all cases. In addition, a captial level will be introduced for those institutions seeking authorisation from the Bank of England. The minimum level will be £1 million, with £5 million for those seeking description as a 'bank'. There will likely be a transitional period to phrase in these latter measures.

Under the Act a deposit protection scheme was set up, to which all recognised banks and licensed deposit-taking institutions are required to contribute. The protection scheme extends to 75% of the first £10,000 held by a depositor in a failed institution.

The Bank of England supervises the banks by monitoring their ongoing liquidity in capital adequacy ratios. The guidelines as to what constitutes prudent levels are revised from time to time, in conjunction with those of other central banks to ensure a similarity of approach. These measures are being extended to include off-balance-sheet items, which can greatly affect a bank's overall exposure profile.

The technique of controlling credit and the money supply alters from time to time. Since September 1981, all banks in the monetary sector are required to hold 0.5% of their eligible liabilities (ELs) in interest-free non-operational accounts at the Bank of England, save those banks with ELs below £10 million. Eligible liabilities were redefined at that time. In establishing a bank's ELs, the bank can offset against its total liabilities funds lent by one institution to another in one monetary sector (i.e. the interbank money market) and money at call placed with money brokers or secured against gilts, treasury or local authority bills and eligible bank bills. The Bank of England does not (but retains the right to) issue a minimum lending rate. Instead it seeks to keep short-term interest rates within an unpublished band through its bill dealings with the discount houses. As a result there has been an increase in the number of banks eligible to discount acceptances with the Bank of England. To ensure market efficiency, these banks must maintain an average of between 2.5% and 5% of their ELs in the form of secured loans with the discount market.

Clearing systems

The clearing system came into being in London during the second half of the eighteenth century. The clearing banks are members of the clearing-houses for cheques and money transfers based in London, Edinburgh and

Belfast. Any other institution is obliged to clear its cheques and transfers through a clearing bank acting as its agent with the Bank of England. The London clearing banks stand at the heart of the banking system. The three Scottish and four Northern Ireland banks perform the same functions in their jurisdictions.

There are two cheque clearings operated in London each business day – the country clearing and town clearing systems. The difference between the two relates to the time it takes for the cheque to clear and good value for the funds to be received.

A town cheque is designated by the initial 'T' after the bank sort code in the top right-hand corner of the cheque. If there is no 'T', it is a cheque drawn on a bank outside the City of London (the 'Square Mile'). (See illustrations.)

A town cheque can be cleared 'for value' the same day, i.e. it is negotiable to receive same-day value funds, if it is for a sum in excess of £10,000. Some cheques for smaller amounts, or indeed a large-sum denominated country cheque, may be cleared under special clearing terms, although same-day value will not necessarily be guaranteed.

Country cheques normally take between two and three days to clear and the funds credited to the customer's account. For corporate clients this can be reduced to one day.

Until recently the number of clearing banks was restricted. However, membership of the Clearing Houses Association has been expanded to include Standard Chartered Bank plc and Citibank NA.

The clearing banks have a large retail network through which they take in deposits, make loans and transfer money on their clients' behalf. There

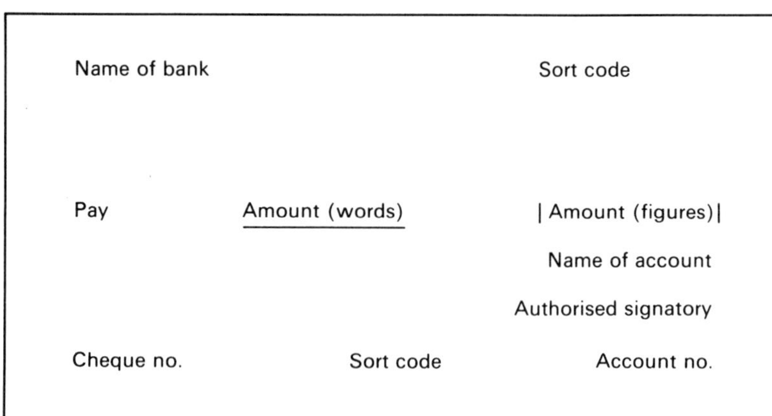

'Country' cheque.

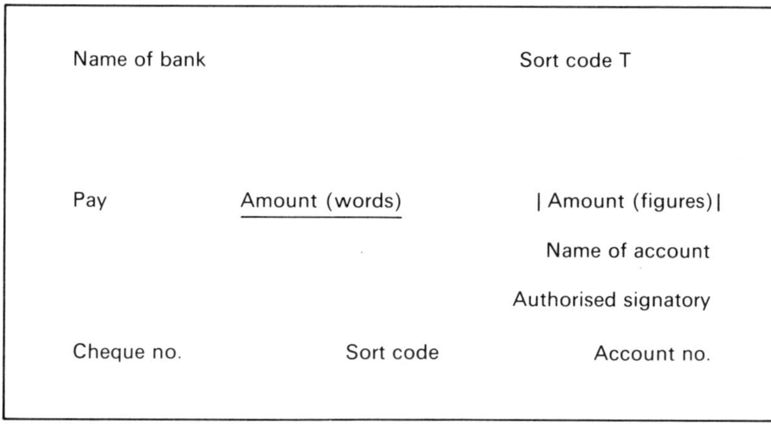

'Town' cheque.

are different types of account that a customer may have for depositing or borrowing funds. The most common is the overdraft account. This account, with a negotiated borrowing limit to it, is technically a demand account. However, it is common practice for the banks to review these accounts annually and 'roll' them forward. For prime customers the interest rate margin would typically be 1% over the bank's own base rate. For smaller companies and the individual a margin of between 3% and 5% is more usual. Interest is calculated on the daily outstanding balance and is paid quarterly in arrears, although some large customers can negotiate semi-annual payments. The overdraft is flexible, particularly if the company is a continual borrower. However, if the balance occasionally becomes positive the customer may lose out since the credit interest payable by the banks in this case is a proportion of their base rate, or a low flat rate. The company should manage its accounts to stay in overdraft and invest surplus funds elsewhere.

Wholesale system

The wholesale banking system is the interbank money market. It is the institutional market in that there are only professional participants. Some large corporates interface directly with the market to borrow or to invest funds, but they may also deal either through a broker or with a customer liaison dealer at a bank. The network of institutions involved centres ultimately through the clearing banks to the Bank of England in the case of money transactions, or through the banks (acceptance houses) and discount houses in the case of acceptance credit (paper) transactions.

Traditionally, acceptance houses were associated with the acceptance of negotiable instruments such as trade bills by endorsing the back of each bill. Thus the bill could be discounted at a discount house and the money made available at once to the other party to the bill. There is an Accepting Houses Committee to which most of the top merchant banks belong.

The discount market, which comprises ten discount houses, is the intermediary through which the Bank of England intervenes in the money markets. Its role is therefore vital. Each week the discount houses bid for the whole of the Treasury bill issue. The bank controls the market by deciding whether to sell the bills at the rates bid, and the amount to sell at the bid.

Exchange control

Exchange controls in the United Kingdom were abolished in 1979, and the law relating to exchange controls taken off the statute books in 1987. There is therefore free exchange of sterling into and out of the country.

UNITED STATES

Central bank, regulatory and monetary control

The United States has a structured and complex banking system. US banks can apply for a charter under federal or state law. State chartered banks are monitored by the state banking authority, while the federal banks are overseen by the Office of the Controller of Currency. The Federal Reserve has specific responsibilities in monitoring its licensed member banks (both state and federal), US bank holding companies, and 'Edge Act' banks – those restricted from undertaking domestic banking operations but still subject to supervision by the Federal Reserve. Banks apply for membership of the Federal Reserve in order to be part of the clearing system and have access to Fed Funds (same-day funds).

The reason for the number of banks and the complex structure of the system is that the McFadden Act 1934, combined with the Bank Holding Company Act 1956, confined US banks' operations to one state only. Within some states there are further restrictions as to the number of branches allowed or geographical spread within the state itself. This situation is slowly changing due to the number of bank failures. Regional grouping of banks is allowed is some areas, but the large money-centre banks have been excluded from participating in the main. Banks do have representative offices, widely spread throughout the country; while these cannot offer the full range of banking services, and in particular cannot take deposits, they can arrange international lines of credit and funding programmes.

Monetary control is maintained by the Federal Reserve System. The Open Market Trading Desk at the New York Federal Reserve Bank, colloquially known as the Fed, executes the directives of the Federal Open Market Committee. This committee meets monthly and its members represent the 12 regional Federal Reserve Banks. The minutes of the committee are released to the public in general after each meeting. The Trading Desk is continuously in the market as a buyer or seller depending on the monetary policy objective.

The Fed also acts on behalf of the US Treasury and foreign official institutions. It acts as a 'lender of last resort' to commercial banks, though the Federal Deposit Insurance Corporation (FDIC) covers individual depositors' losses up to US$100,000. For depositors to enjoy this protection the bank where the deposit is placed must be a member of the FDIC.

Clearing system

Originally the system was cumbersome and time-consuming, which gave rise to long float times because of the size of the country, the number of banks and the vagaries of the US mail system. These factors, combined with the fact that the overdraft as such does not exist in the United States, led to the development of speciality payment and collection systems to clear cheques more quickly and cut down idle bank float.

There are three basic payments systems used: cheques, wire transfers, and Automated Clearing House (ACH) or Electronic Funds Transfers (EFT).

Cheques

Cheques are the most common form of payment instrument in use. As a consequence an elaborate, nationwide cheque clearing network exists to guarantee rapid and efficient processing. This involves physical movement of the cheques from the depository bank to the drawee bank, and is largely dependent on couriers and on private and commercial airlines. Uniform numbering of banks by the American Bankers Association in 1910 eased the processing, as did the development of MICR (Magnetic Ink Character Recognition) in 1956, which led to the automated handling of cheques. The encoded line at the bottom of the cheque is machine readable and contains all the information necessary for processing and returning the cheques to the drawee bank.

There are four ways that the cheque might be routed for clearing:

1. Internally within the bank when payer's and payee's accounts are held at the same bank. Funds would have same-day value.
2. Clearing-house presentment, which effectively is a local clearing arrangement between major banks in the same geographical area. Each bank, because it has cheques drawn on others within the same locale and similarly on itself, will present the cheques to the clearing-house, where a netting process will be effected. The resultant net correspondent balances will be debited or credited at the Federal Reserve. There is a series of time deadlines for presentments which will affect when the funds are cleared.
3. Federal Reserve Bank presentations cater for instances where cheques are drawn on banks outside the local area. In this case the Federal Reserve acts as a collection agent for the banks. This clearing can take from same-day to three days.
4. Direct-send presentment allows for high-money-value cheques to be cleared directly, either by sending them to the appropriate Federal Reserve Bank or to the drawee bank. These funds would be available on the same day, or next day.

Some smaller banks use larger ones to collect for them, particularly where the larger bank has a good network of corresponding banks, which will improve clearing times. In these instances the bank would physically present the cheques in bulk to the larger bank for processing.

The key to clearing times is what is known as the availability schedule, which banks produce and which are independently verified. The schedule serves as a timetable indicating when funds will be cleared and therefore available for use.

Wire transfers

Wire transfers are generally used to settle high-value items on a same-day value basis, for instance in securities settlements. The cost of transfer tends to be high but this is offset by the quicker funds availability. Wires are initiated by telephone, telex or via a VDU terminal by the customer to the bank. The bank will transmit the transfer either by Fed wire, CHIPS or SWIFT to the receiving bank, which will in turn credit the company account holder and notify them of a receipt into their account.

The transfer networks all provide same-day funds but their use will be determined by the location of the receiving bank.

Fed wires are used for domestic transfers. It is a Federal Reserve sponsored network. CHIPS (Clearing House Interbank Payment System), on the other hand, is a private network involving about 135 New York City financial institutions, allowing transfer of funds within member banks' accounts. Final settlement is through Federal Reserve accounts. It is operated by the New York Clearing House Association. The third network is SWIFT (Society For Worldwide Interbank Financial Telecommunication), which is an international network used to send standardised transfer instructions from one bank to the other.

Electronic payments

Money can be moved electronically through the Automated Clearing House (ACH). There is a network of 30 Independent Automated Clearing House Associations; in 28 instances the local Federal Reserve Bank processes the transactions. The other two ACHs use separate processors, though ultimately payments are settled through the local Fed. Availability is the next business day.

Essentially, the payment company initiates instructions to the bank using a VDU terminal or magnetic tape. The bank will 'sift' the information for any debits or credits against itself and then route the rest to the appropriate local ACH. This occurs on day one. On receipt the local ACH will sort the information and post the appropriate entries to the Federal Reserve on day two.

This method is inexpensive compared with wire transfer and lends itself to funds concentration through an internal netting system, regular and dividend disbursements, and funding payroll accounts.

As payment systems have been developed so have collection services. The most widely known system is that of the 'lockbox'.

The aim is to accelerate the depositing of funds by sending items straight to the bank and not to the company. The process is as follows:

1. The company is assigned a specific box number, which is used in 'remit to' instructions on its invoices.
2. To expedite the handling of mail at the local post office, the lockbox banks are assigned unique zip codes. The mail is collected by the bank.
3. The mail is then sorted within the bank into box numbers.
4. Most banks organise processing on a batch system basis. According to the company's instructions the mail is opened and the cheques are checked for negotiability. The information on the cheques is then coded on to the computer. This coding is separately checked to verify the information.
5. The cheques are then processed for collection by pre-sorting into drawee bank locations. This will assign availability of cleared funds to the items, which will be posted to the company's account.
6. Finally, the cheques are routed through the most efficient cheque clearing system to ensure availability times are met. This entails shipping the cheques by air/courier service to the drawee banks.

The company can receive a range of information regarding the lockbox activity, in paper form, by mail or courier, or electronically. The service can be tailored. It is an expensive service, despite automation wherever possible, but this is relative to the accelerated deposit time of cheques. Many banks have specialised in providing lockbox services, in particular the mid-western banks, which due to their location tend to have shorter mail float times compared with those on the west or east coast. Some banks have set up regional lockbox centres to fine tune the process further; cheques will be picked up from the local post office and physically couriered (normally by air) to the main processing centre.

There are many configurations, as each bank will seek the speediest method of processing and clearing cheques applicable to its location.

Wholesale system

The participants in the US money markets are numerous, ranging from federal agencies to the large money-centre banks, international banks, investment banks, brokers, institutions and corporates. The largest player is the Federal Reserve System. The wholesale system in New York is largely securitised, in that investments are made in return for paper representing the borrower's commitment to pay on maturity. The form of interbank cash market that exists in London is therefore limited in New York.

The largest corporate debt market is the commercial paper market. In this market five or six major investment banks act as dealers in issuing paper and selling it to corporate investors or banking institutions. To aid the investor in choosing among different corporate risks a rating system exists. The two main rating agencies are Moodys, and Standard and Poors. Their rating tables indicate the differentiation of the creditworthiness of corporate issuers, which in turn leads to a differential in the investment yields offered to the investor.

In competition for investors' funds is the US government. The sale of its debt instruments – Treasury bills, government notes and bonds of varying maturities, and federal agency debt instruments – dominates the market.

The Treasury issues securities, marketable or non-marketable, under the authority of the Second Liberty Bond Act 1917. Under this Act Congress can limit the outstanding total face value of securities issued. This limit is raised by Congress from time to time to accommodate the government's funding requirements. In recent years this limit has been raised annually, in the face of the mounting US budget deficit problem.

Marketable securities, being bills, notes and bonds, differ only in length of period to maturity at the time of issuance, save that bills are sold on a discount basis while the others carry a coupon. These securities are acceptable to secure deposits of public monies, and as security for notes discounted or rediscounted at the Federal Reserve.

Formerly all securities, whether in bearer or registered form, were physically issued on paper. This is no longer the case as electronic 'book entry' is now the norm to register ownership of a security.

The government has laid down procedures regarding its funding pattern. Prior to each quarter it announces the total re-funding package. The Treasury debt is then sold at auction, in accordance with the issuance pattern.

Type of borrowing	Auction pattern	Comments
Treasury bills (discounted)		
(i) 3 month and 6 month bills	weekly	
(ii) 52 week bills	every 4 weeks	
(iii) Cash management bills (maturities up to 6 months)	irregular	issued when government borrowing heaviest, raises new cash
Coupon issues		
(i) 2 year notes	monthly	
(ii) 3 year notes	mid-qtr	(Feb., May, Aug., Nov.)
(iii) 4 year notes	end of qtr mth	(Mar., June, Sept., Dec.)
(iv) 5 year notes	beginning qtr mth	(Mar., June, Sept., Dec.)
(v) 7 year notes	end mth of qtr	
(vi) 10 year notes	mid-qtr	(Feb., May, Aug., Nov.)
(vii) Foreign targeted notes (FTNS)	irregular	raises new cash, sold only to foreign institutions
(viii) Bonds – maturities 15, 20 or 30 yrs	mid-qtr	(Feb., May, Aug., Nov.)

The main characteristic in the US wholesale system is the depth of the secondary markets in traded securities, exceptions being commercial paper and bankers' acceptances – though the latter are eligible for sale to the Fed under a repurchase agreement or on its own account.

Exchange control

There is none in existence regarding the exchange of the US dollar for capital or trading purposes.

CANADA

Central bank, regulatory and monetary control

The central bank, established in 1935, is the Bank of Canada. This institution, along with the Inspector General of Banks, administers the

Bank Act. The Canadians tend to revise their banking law every ten years or so to keep it in line with current practice and prevailing economic and social conditions. The last revision was in 1980. The banking industry is highly regulated, with procedures stipulating all facets of banking practice.

The Bank, whose head office is in Ottawa, has the sole right to issue paper money. It plays a key role domestically in the payment (clearing) system. This role was clarified when the Canadian Payments Association (CPA) was set up in 1980. The Bank is the provider of the final means of settlement between participants in the national clearing and settlement system. This is through its agencies across the country, and in its role as the clearer to the government. Its regional agencies are in Halifax, Saint John, Montreal, Toronto, Winnipeg, Regina, Calgary and Vancouver.

Monetary policy is established by the Bank in response to international conditions and the domestic economic situation. Typically the method of raising or reducing interest rates is the mechanism used to regulate monetary expansion. However, the Bank does buy or sell the Canadian dollar in the currency markets as an alternative means of stabilising the currency, particularly versus the closest trading ally, the US dollar.

A scheme of depositor's insurance was set up under the Canadian Deposit Insurance Corporation Act and the Quebec Deposit Insurance Act. This scheme provides insurance to a maximum of C$60,000 per depositor in each bank.

Clearing system

Significant advances were made in the clearing system by the establishment of the Canadian Payments Association in 1980. The objectives were to set up and operate a national clearing and settlement system and to plan a national payment system. The CPA is a private association of interested parties. Its management and operation are the responsibility of a board of directors. The director is appointed by the Bank of Canada, but its members are elected by the CPA's member organisations. Previously the clearing system was operated through the chartered banks. Any other institution had to use the services of one of the chartered banks as its agent in clearing customer cheques through the system. This situation has been simplified as non-bank deposit-taking institutions now rank equally with the chartered banks. The criterion allowing a non-chartered bank to become a direct clearer in the system is that its volume of transactions must account for 0.5% of the total volume of cheques, money orders and transfers in the Canadian clearing system. There are currently 13 direct clearers in addition to the central bank. They exchange and clear among themselves at ten regional centres from coast to coast and so shorten the time taken for cheques to clear.

In July 1986 the system effectively became a same-day system as entries in the books at the Bank of Canada, which reflect the previous day's net clearing gain or loss by each direct clearer, were retroactively dated. In other words, the value is transferred among the institutions on the same business day as the underlying transactions take place.

Wholesale system

The financial system in Canada includes a number of different types of intermediary deposit-taking institutions. The primary type is the chartered bank.

Chartered banks are analogous to commercial banks in other countries. Although originally established to serve the commercial, governmental and industrial sectors, they now encompass the retail and personal financial sectors too. The five largest banks are nationwide, though the majority are regional or sector-based.

All chartered banks are incorporated and operate under the terms of the Bank Act. They can accept various types of deposit, hold securities portfolios, make loans, deal in foreign exchange, and so forth.

Other deposit-taking institutions, which tend to be more specialised in their operation, are co-operative institutions (including local credit unions), trust and mortgage loan companies, and governmental savings offices.

Exchange control

There are no exchange control requirements.

JAPAN

Central bank, regulatory and monetary control

The central bank is the Bank of Japan which, with the Ministry of Finance, presides over the banking sector. Banking licences are issued by the Ministry of Finance. The legal requirements for establishing and performing banking operations were set down in the Banking Law of 1981.

The Bank of Japan was established in 1892. The administrative section of the Bank is called the policy board, which is comprised of the president of the Bank of Japan, representatives from the Ministry of Finance and the Economic Planning Agency, and four representatives from commerce.

The Bank issues currency, the amount of note issuance being determined by the Minister of Finance. It is also banker to the banks, and transacts loans and deposits with them. As banker to the government it accepts bonds and bills and acts as the government's fiscal agent.

The Bank therefore carries out financial policies such as lending, which consists of determining the official discount rate and the lending limit system. It transacts open market operations in order to control the volume of available money. It also sets levels of reserve deposit limits, which are balances that the banks are required to hold with the Central Bank, in order to regulate the volume of credit facilities made available to customers by certain finanical institutions. In addition to the formal methods of control, the Bank uses moral persuasion ('window guidance') on an individual bank basis, similar to that of the Bank of England.

In 1981 an 'Extraordinary Lending Rate System' was introduced as an emergency measure should there be a sudden inflow into the country of short-term funds, which could disturb the currency and money markets.

The banking system consists of the central bank and three other types of institution:

1. Private financial institutions, split between commercial banks, specialised financial institutions and others, such as insurance companies.
2. Government financial institutions, such as the Export–Import Bank and the Development Bank, and public corporations for enterprise loans, housing and agricultural finance.
3. Governmental institutions, such as the postal savings scheme.

In total there are some 7,700 organisations, including all the credit associations and agricultural co-operatives. Foreign exchange is routed through one institution, the Bank of Tokyo.

Clearing system

Banking business is similar to that of commercial banks in Europe and the United States.

Deposits are the major source of operating funds for ordinary banks, and there is intense competition between the banks vying for business. Deposits are classified as demand or time. No interest is paid on demand deposits, so companies tend to keep only small balances against which cheques, bills and notes can be drawn. The next category of deposit is the ordinary deposit, which is also on a demand basis but on which interest is paid. As in Europe, a wide variety of deposit accounts is available.

There is a deposit insurance system covering banks, long-term credit banks, foreign exchange banks, credit associations and co-operatives. A premium of eight-thousandths of total deposits held is paid by the institution to the Insurance Corporation. The limit of insurance payment is three million yen per depositor.

For payments, individuals tend to use cash, though cheque services do exist. In the main, direct debit or credit card systems prevail.

Companies use promissory notes or cheques in settling payments. The former tend to be used for stock purchases, the latter for daily payments. The promissory note system is similar to that of the bill of exchange. For clearing, the bank initially sorts the items before sending for collection. There are 179 local clearing-houses throughout Japan that handle collections in their areas. Remote collections are handled by the domestic exchange system. Final clearing between the institutions is made through accounts held at the Bank of Japan.

Wholesale system

The Tokyo money market consists of the yen call market, the foreign currency call market, the bill discount market and Gensaki market.

Participants in the yen call market are called Tanshi companies (money market dealers), e.g. banks, insurance and securities companies and other financial institutions. Institutions borrow or lend the excess in monitoring their reserve accounts at the Bank of Japan for half-days in the yen call market. This can be on an 'unconditional' basis, i.e. overnight loans which will continue automatically until closed out, or for a fixed period up to seven days. The latter are collateralised by designated bonds, notes or stocks. Interest accrued is paid monthly on rollover overnight loans, but at maturity on fixed loans.

The foreign currency call market is also called the Tokyo dollar core market, as most transactions are in US dollars. Tanshi companies act as brokers. Only authorised foreign exchange banks are permitted to participate. Foreign currency balances are lent/borrowed generally for periods up to a month.

The Bank of Japan participates in the bill discount market along with banks and securities companies, with the Tanshi companies acting as dealers. The bill market comprises banks' own acceptances, collateralised by loan or trade notes for maturities between one and four months.

Gensaki transactions are sale/purchases of Japanese government bonds and bank debentures under buy-back/sell-back arrangements (the repurchase market). All the major types of institution participate.

Exchange control

In 1980 exchange controls were abolished to allow the free use of yen. Some borrowings in yen by non-residents are subject to approval, though none is required where (a) funds are to be used by the company raising them; (b) where the borrowing is for less than one year; (c) where the borrowing is for one to five years but in an amount less than Y200 million; and (d) where the borrowing is over five years but less than Y100 million.

GERMANY

Central bank, regulatory and monetary control

The Deutsche Bundesbank is the central bank of the Federal Republic of Germany. Its head office is in Frankfurt with a main branch in each of the 11 states, known as Landeszentralbanken, and some 200 branches throughout the country. The president of each Landeszentralbank, together with the governors of the Bundesbank, comprise the policy-making body of the central bank. Its responsibilities are to maintain monetary stability and to support the economic policy of the federal government. In 1961, under the Banking Act, the Federal Banking Supervisory Board was established. This body implements central bank law – which defines the supervision and inspection of banks, as well as information requirements and capital, liquidity and management criteria.

The Bundesbank acts as sole issuer of banknotes, intermediary for interbank transactions, lender of last resort, and banker to the government. Its main task, however, is to regulate the monetary supply in order to maintain the value of the Deutschmark and the amount of credit available in the banking system.

There are two main ways of accomplishing this. The first is by fixing the discount rate, through which the Bundesbank refinances the institutions. The second is by setting the Lombard Rate, which is normally 1% or 2% above the discount rate. This rate is applicable to the Lombard loans, for which Treasury bills and fixed-interest securities are pledged to the central bank for a period of up to three months. The Bank influences the money market through an open market policy, i.e. by buying or selling Treasury instruments at certain rates. Another mechanism is to alter the level of non-interest-bearing deposits that each credit institution must maintain with the Bundesbank. Levels and types of deposit vary according to the size of the organisation.

The Federal Banking Supervisory Board, located in West Berlin, has authority to issue and withdraw banking licences, establish capital and liquidity ratios, approve senior bank appointments, request information and conduct investigations.

Clearing systems

The bulk of domestic clearing, remittance and bill collection is settled through the Bundesbank and its 203 branches. In towns where there is a branch, local daily clearing is offered whereby the Bundesbank branch determines the clearing balance of each bank and debits or credits its central bank account as appropriate.

Where institutions do not take part in the local clearing, transfers between Bundesbank branches are arranged. The central bank automated giro system can be used to access any bank in the Federal Republic. There are similar giro networks set up by the savings banks and co-operative banks.

Payments are typically cashless, in the form of direct debits or credit transfers. Cheques are not as popular in Germany as in other areas of Europe, partly due to the preference for credit transfers.

Wholesale system

The structure of German banking is a mixed one, having developed over time. As mentioned above, the centre of the system is the Bundesbank and Landeszentralbanken. Then there are specialist and retail banks, differentiated according to the types of service they offer to their customers and the types of deposit they attract. The larger sector of multi-purpose banks offering customers a 'full service' are of three types: commercial banks (private commercial banks), including the foreign and regional banks; savings banks (Sparkasse) and their central institutions (Girozentralen); and co-operative banks, with their central institutions being either urban (Volksbanken) or agricultural (Raiffeisen) based.

There are a number of specialised banks such as mortgage banks, the instalment credit institutions, security deposit banks, and so on.

The two most widely used forms of short-term credit are current account overdrafts and bill discounting. The former is usually priced at a margin over central bank rates. The latter, in order to obtain fine rates, must be rediscountable at the Bundesbank. The terms are that they must be of prime quality, be issued for trade purposes, and mature within 90 days.

Exchange control

There are no exchange control restrictions. The Deutschmark floats freely, though it is a member of the European Monetary System.

FRANCE

Central bank, regulatory and monetary control

The Bank of France is the central bank. Like other central banks it monitors the banking system, issues legal tender and plays the central role in the clearing system. Supervision of the system is by the finance ministry. It plays an important role in policy decisions regarding regulatory monetary control, including exchange controls. A series of committees, of different constituents, are involved in the process of supervision. The central committee is the Conseil National du Crédit (CNC), which has 51 members representing banking, commerce and industry. It is a consultative body, with wide powers.

The committee that issues banking licences is called the Établissement de Crédit committee. The definition of an Établissement de Crédit was laid down in 1984 when the new Banking Law came into effect. The description refers to a legal entity whose main business is to carry out banking operations, such as taking deposits, lending and so forth. There are two broad categories of the Établissement de Crédit. The first includes those institutions authorised to accept deposits with a maturity of up to two years, such as universal banks and co-operative banks. The second tier of institutions differs only in that they require further authorisation before they can take deposits, e.g. finance companies and specialised financical bodies.

The rules and decisions of the licensing committee are watched over by a general banking regulation committee, the Commission Bancaire. It is composed of six members, the chairman being the Governor of the Bank of France.

In line with other central banks, the Bank of France is empowered to introduce ratio requirements and revise rules regarding liquidity and capital adequacy. There are various credit supervision requirements with which the banks have to comply.

Clearing system

The present system is dominated by domestic clearing, where the use of the cheque as a method of payment predominates. The system is similar to those of other European countries, with the ultimate netting between banks being effected through accounts held at the Bank of France and its network of 234 branches.

Because of the cost of processing cheques, the banks have moved to introduce automatic cash dispensers which give access to all banks in the system.

Wholesale system

Prior to the 1984 redefinition of banks, there were three types of bank: banques de dépôts, banques d'affaires and banques de crédit à long et moyen terme. French banking business was split between the three; however, the distinctions have now gone, and a general banking licence is granted entitling an institution to carry out all banking operations.

Banks source themselves from demand and savings deposits, and by offering non-negotiable certificates of deposit and savings certificates of up to five years' maturity. Lending is predominantly paper-based, against bills of exchange or promissory notes. Lending rates are by reference to the banks' base rate.

In the money market, transactions are carried out through brokerage houses. The interbank market is based on unsecured loans. The Bank of France oversees the market and from the time to time will take part in open market activities.

Exchange control

During 1986/87 the Bank of France has sought to relax the bulk of exchange controls. Internationally the French franc floats freely, though it is within the European Monetary System.

THE NETHERLANDS

Central bank, regulatory and monetary control

The De Nederlandsche Bank is the country's central bank and sole issuer of banknotes. Its main office is in Amsterdam. Under the terms of the Act on the Supervision of the Credit System, the Bank has been given powers to authorise and supervise licensed credit institutions.

Licences are given only if an institution complies with certain conditions relating to monetary resources, control practices and management depth. The supervision of these factors is ongoing, particularly that of monetary resources since capital adequacy ratios are carefully monitored.

The Bank also acts as a monetary authority and implements policy. As with other central banks in Europe it manipulates interest rates, and directly intervenes in the foreign exchange markets to stabilise the value of the Dutch guilder. From time to time direct credit control measures are used. The Bank is a licensing authority for foreign exchange transactions. This authority is delegated to the commercial banks, which act as intermediaries in the settlement of international payments.

Clearing system

The central bank is the banker's bank, since it acts as the clearing bank for all domestic payments. It is also the lender of last resort.

The system of clearing is very similar to those of other European countries. However, because the giro system is very efficient, cheques are seldom used in settlement of debts. Using the postal giro system (PCGD), the customer has a numbered account and a book of preprinted transfer forms used to effect payments. Security is maintained in that loss of the forms means a transfer will not be effected.

Wholesale system

The commercial banks in the Netherlands constitute the largest group of banks as they provide the bulk of lending to the industrial sector. They concentrate in the main on short-term lending such as overdrafts, medium-term lending, factoring, leasing and so forth. Most lending by banks is on a secured basis, such as through a mortgage, debt assignment or transfer of title on current assets, though possession of the last remains with the company. Unlike the case in Germany, bill discounting is not popular because the money market is cash- rather than paper-orientated. Any bills issued, say in connection with export financing, will most likely be held in the bank's portfolio as there is no secondary paper market. A Dutch commercial paper market has now been established but this is small relative to business sector requirements.

Rabobanks are the specialised agricultural credit banks, formed into a co-operative. Their activities are similar to those of the commercial banks, though their customers tend to live outside the towns.

Other specialist banks include the Post Office Savings Bank and other private savings banks, the mortgage banks, finance companies and so forth.

Exchange control

The Dutch guilder is part of the European Monetary System. There are no exchange controls regarding loans taken up from non-residents, though the central bank has to be notified of direct investments (equity). There are no controls on repatriating earnings abroad, nor are there exchange controls on imports and exports.

BELGIUM

Central bank, regulatory and monetary control

Bank legislation is governed by the Bank Act 1935 and Mammoth Act 1975. The former segregated commercial investment banking, while the latter imposed a two-tiered board structure.

The regulatory bodies controlling the system are the Bank of Belgium and the Banking Commission. They work in close co-operation with the Minister of Finance to ensure a similarity of purpose.

The Bank of Belgium, or National Bank as it is also called, acts as lender of last resort, issues currency and monitors monetary policy. It maintains the latter, after consultation with its co-bodies, mainly through control of the rediscount bill market, by granting short-term current account advances, and by credit control and interest rate influences. The Banking Commission performs a dual role: that of supervising the banks and, separately, that of centralising information issued by organisations during public offerings. It is the licensing authority of banks.

The Rediscount and Deposit Insurance Agency (RGI) protects depositors against bank failures. It has a special role in that banks can present short-dated bills for rediscount. The RGI has an important role in maintaining short-term liquidity in the system.

There is monetary union between Belgium and Luxembourg. The role of supervising exchange control of money movements has been entrusted to the Belgo-Luxembourg Exchange Institute (BLEI), which has authority over both countries. In fact the day-to-day management is carried out by the National Bank.

Clearing system

In 1974 a national clearing system was set up, using standardised customer account numbers for all financial intermediaries. This has greatly enhanced the use of electronic funds clearing, particularly important due to the high density of banks in the country.

Customers can negotiate overdraft facilities, normally charged at a percentage over the banks' base rate, for day-to-day funding requirements. The domestic commercial bill market is well developed, the discounts charged depending on buyers' or suppliers' quality.

Wholesale system

There are three main types of bank, which formerly were distinct in the types of facilities they offered. However, the edges are now somewhat blurred. They are commercial banks, the private banks and the public credit institutions.

The commercial banks offer the widest range of facilities in the retail and wholesale markets, from straight deposits and chequing arrangements to overdrafts and medium-term loans. The private savings banks principally take deposits against which they lend mortgage funds. Their business tends to be domestic rather than international.

Public credit institutions were set up to fill gaps left by the private banks. The first was the taking in of small deposits from the private investor. This role was filled by the General Savings and Pensions Bank (GSPB). The second role was that of granting medium- and long-term finance, filled by the National Industrial Credit Organisation. The third was the regional gap, filled by the Communal Credit of Belgium Bank. The last acts as banker to the local municipalities, and has a role in funding long-term projects.

Exchange control

There are two exchange markets:

1. The official exchange market, known as convertible Belgian francs, used for imports and exports of goods, etc.
2. The free exchange market, known as financial Belgian francs, used for bond and share transactions, etc.

Both 'currencies' float freely; the convertible franc is within the European Monetary System. There are no foreign exchange restrictions.

ITALY

Central bank, regulatory and monetary control

The banking system in Italy is complex and is currently under review. In essence the basic provisions governing the banking sector are set down in the Banking Law of 1936. Supervision is split between the Inter-Ministerial Committee for Credit and Savings (the CICR) and the Bank of Italy, the central bank.

The CICR is the regulatory body for monitoring credit and savings institutions, whereas the Bank of Italy monitors the banking system itself. The Bank also issues banknotes and is responsible for managing the Treasury's liquidity position and open market operations. The Bank has wide legislative powers in connection with supervision of banks within the system. The central bank information requirements are extensive, as is the degree to which the Bank is involved with banks and companies since all new shares, bonds and debentures must be authorised by the Bank in advance. Monetary control is managed by the Bank through its rediscount operations, general advances, reserve adjustment and so forth.

There is a range of banks contributing to the banking sector:

1. Public charter banks are State-owned banks, their charters having been approved by the Treasury minister and the boards appointed by the government.
2. National interest banks are established in the form of joint-stock companies. They have to operate in at least 30 provinces, and must be classified as being of 'public interest'. The majority of their capital is held by the Industrial Reconstruction Institute, though their shares are listed on the stock exchange.
3. Credit banks tend to be private banks, although formed in a similar manner to the joint-stock banks.
4. Co-operative banks' capital structure is fragmented. No shareholder may own more than L7.5 million of the capital if it is less than L500 million, but if the capital is greater than the maximum then the maximum holding rises to L15 million. The banks are typically local.
5. Pledge banks are recognised by decree of the Minister of the Treasury as corporate entities.
6. Others include a range of local banking co-operatives and associations, and the foreign banks.

Clearing system

In operation, the clearing system, within Italy is similar to that operated in other European countries, although there is a growing emphasis on the use of electronic cash dispensers, 'Bancomat'. The payment system is overseen by the Central Bank.

Wholesale system

The interbank market is well developed in Italy, based on overnight deposits, term deposits and certificates of deposit. The last can be issued by a bank for a maturity of six to 18 months.

Interbank deposits are exempt from the reserve requirements of the Bank of Italy but a 25% withholding tax is applied on interest.

Exchange control

The lira is within the European Monetary System. Authorisation is required if residents (companies) intend to borrow abroad, though direct investments may be made by foreigners. There are no restrictions on repatriation of funds.

Proceeds of exports must be surrendered to the banking system in return for local currency.

SWEDEN

Central bank, regulatory and monetary control

The Swedish central bank, the Bank of Sweden, is the oldest such in the world, having been founded in 1668. It is a national institution, subordinate to the Riksdag. The Riksdag is the legislative branch of the Swedish government as well as its policy-making body.

The functions of the Bank of Sweden are similar to those of other central banks: to issue notes, administer the country's official reserves, act as banker and lender of last resort, and manage the clearing centre. The most important task is the execution of monetary policy. This is done by directive and by law. The most widely used methods are discount rate setting, open market operations, and imposition of liquidity or cash ratios on the banks.

The licensing and supervision of the banks is done through the Bank Inspection Board. The Board issues new bank charters (licences) for ten years, but they can be withdrawn if the bank does not conduct its affairs properly. The government has sought ways to tighten its monitoring control over the banking sector, not only by widening the powers of the Board but also by insisting on government-appointed directors, and approved chairmen, on the central boards of the commercial banks.

Clearing system

Domestic clearing and indeed the foreign payment system are almost exclusively handled by the commercial banks, the postal giro and a few savings banks. The system is typical of many others, allowing cheque clearing through any bank. However, the whole payment process is rapidly becoming automated in line with other countries.

Wholesale system

Besides the central bank there are three types of bank: commercial, savings, and co-operative banks. Banking legislation in 1969 widened the scope of operation for these banks, thus making them more homogeneous.

Generally, the commercial banks are not allowed to offer facilities of more than one year, though this has been eased. To alleviate the situation the banks give evergreen rollover loans of one year that are automatically renewable, hence becoming medium- or long-term in nature. The banks assist in long-term financing by acting as underwriters to stock issues on the stock market; however, they are not allowed to hold stock to their own order.

The traditional role of the savings banks is to promote personal savings. The banks have formed a co-operative central bank, the Sparbankernas Bank, which is a commercial bank in its own right. The loan portfolio of the savings bank is chiefly long-term funding of housing and agriculture.

The co-operative banks were first formed to provide banking services for the farming sector, but this role has been extended to include all types of customer. Their structure is akin to a pyramid with a central administrative body, the Federation of Swedish Co-operative Banks, at the top. Below this there is a commercial bank, the Foreningsbankernas Bank, which acts as a central bank to the subsequent tiers of co-operative banks – of which there were 400,000 at the end of 1984.

The money markets have developed rapidly over the past few years, as they have been liberated to allow the trading of primary and secondary paper.

Exchange control

Foreign exchange is subject to control exercised by the Swedish central bank. The value of the krona is related to a trade-weighted basket of 15 major currencies. Dealing may only be through authorised banks.

SWITZERLAND

Central bank, regulatory and monetary control

The central bank is the Swiss National Bank, though the Swiss banking system is supervised by the Federal Banking Commission. It in turn has delegated its authority to external auditors. All banks are monitored, particularly their capital ratios. This supervision is extended to finance companies if they solicit the public for deposits.

The Banking Law of Switzerland provides for the creation of hidden reserves. This is to allow unexpected losses to be absorbed without disturbing investor confidence in the banks. However, the use of this practice is restricted by the central bank.

The banking sector is a mix between private and publicly owned banks, the latter including cantonal and local savings banks.

Clearing system

Switzerland, in line with other countries, is moving to cashless forms of payment for goods and services, although the cheque payment system is widely used by individuals. The system itself is supervised by the Central Bank, through which the net balances are cleared.

Wholesale system

The interbank money market is small in that there are few instruments to be traded and few participants. The development of the market has been impeded by the imposition of stamp duty of between 0.15% and 0.30%, regardless of maturity or whether the debtor is resident or non-resident. In essence there is no short-term paper in issuance, as the international money market transactions of the Swiss banks serve as a substitute for the domestic market.

An important element of short-term transactions are those associated with fiduciary accounts. These are off-balance-sheet deposits of a bank for the account and risk of the customer with respect to the currency, transfer and credit risk. These accounts are exempt for withholding tax purposes. The banks act as intermediaries in placing the funds worldwide.

Exchange control

There are no exchange control restrictions.

AUSTRALIA

Central bank, regulatory and monetary control

The regulatory framework under the supervision of the reserve bank of Australia, the central bank, was established under the Banking Act 1959. Since then there have been a number of review studies undertaken to improve the efficiency of the financial sector. This has led to some deregulation and liberalisation in the system. The key elements were: the floating of the Australian dollar and removal of exchange controls; expansion of the foreign exchange market; removal of maturity restrictions on bank deposits; the abolition of certain interest rate lending controls; and in particular the granting of additional banking licences to new domestic and foreign-owned banks, which has more than doubled the number of banks operating in Australia.

The central bank's role is like that of many others in that it is the issuer of notes, the lender of last resort and the banker's bank. It also supervises banks authorised under the Banking Act, based on an assessment of the adequacy of management systems regarding risk exposure, on capital adequacy criteria and similarly liquidity adequacy, and on monitoring off-balance-sheet activity.

The reserve bank maintains close ties with its co-central banks around the world, particularly with regard to monitoring prudent banking practices.

It should be noted that the supervision of non-bank financial institutions (NBFIs) is carried out by other state or commonwealth authorities. NBFIs developed when banking sector growth was inhibited by official regulation; they include institutions such as building societies, finance companies, credit unions and merchant banks.

Clearing system

This is similar to other payment clearing systems, where net interbank balances are settled through the central bank. As elsewhere there is also a growing tendency to move to paperless transfers.

Automated payments by the consumer as well as the business user are more widespread. This has been a feature of cost and geography, similar to Canadian developments.

Wholesale system

Until relatively recently the Australian wholesale market was largely domestic in its orientation. As the Australian dollar was floated and exchange controls lifted, international factors began to have a bearing. This led in time to new authorised banks and the setting up of a futures exchange and commercial paper market, all of which serve to increase liquidity and depth in the wholesale market.

The primary instrument is still the bank bill, upon which most lending is based, but the straight loan market is being established on the back of the developing interbank market. Most consumer and corporate short-term credit is handled on overdraft accounts through the four main retail banks.

Exchange control

As already noted, there are no exchange control restrictions.

Glossary

Accounting exposure. See Translation exposure

Appreciation. The gradual increase in the value of a currency, usually occurring over several days or weeks as the result of market forces of supply and demand in a system of floating exchange rates. By contrast, an up valuation (or revaluation) is an official government act which produces a substantial increase in the exchange rate, usually overnight.

Arbitrage. Purchase of securities or commodities in one market for immediate resale in another in order to profit from a price discrepancy; or taking advantage of divergences in the exchange rates in different money markets by buying a currency in one market and selling it in another.

Back-to-back financing. An intracorporate loan channelled through a bank.

Balance of payments. A financial statement prepared for a given country summarising the flows of goods, services and funds between the residents of the country and the rest of the world during a certain period of time.

Balance of trade. The net of imports and exports of goods and services reported in the balance of payments.

Balance sheet exposure. See Translation exposure.

Balloon payment. The simultaneous return of principal and interest on a loan at the end of the loan period (on the maturity date).

Bank draft. A draft addressed to the bank.

Banker's acceptance. A customer bill drawn on a bank and accepted (i.e. endorsed and backed with its guarantee to pay) by the bank with the bank's commitment to honour the bill. The instrument is then a marketable security which can normally be sold in the money market.

Base. The local currency in terms of foreign exchange quotations, which are normally non-base/base, i.e. the amount of base currency required to purchase/sell one unit of foreign currency; the most notable exception is sterling, which is quoted base/non-base.

Bear. A trader who expects a currency to become weaker and sells forward currency expecting to make a profit on the exchange.

Bear market. A market with pessimistic investors.

Bid rate. The price at which the crediting party is prepared to purchase a currency or accept a deposit.

Bill of exchange. A written order to pay a specified sum of money on a particular date to a named person or to the bearer.

Blocked currency. A currency that is not freely convertible to other currencies due to exchange controls.

Bond. A security which shows the liability of the issuing party. It is usually a negotiable instrument with a fixed maturity date longer than one year.

Break-even exchange rate. The particular spot exchange rate which must prevail at the maturity of deposit or debt in a foreign currency (which has not been covered in the forward market) so that there will be no advantage to any party from interest rate differentials.

Bretton Woods. A meeting of representatives of non-Communist countries in Bretton Woods, New Hampshire in 1944. The participants agreed on the characteristics of the international monetary system which prevailed until 1971. This system was called the Bretton Woods System and was a fixed exchange rate system.

Broker. An individual who introduces the two parties in a transaction to each other.

Brokerage. A charge made by a broker for a service.

Bull. A trader who expects a currency to become firmer and buys forward currency expecting to make a profit on the exchange.

Bull market. A market with optimistic investors.

Business day. A normal business day on which a payment to settle a money market transaction can be made. An eligible value date for a foreign exchange transaction must be a business day in the home countries of both the currencies involved.

Call money. Funds placed with a financial institution without fixed maturity date (i.e. the money can be 'called' or withdrawn at any time).

Capital account. The accounts in the balance of payments which measure the change in liabilities and financial claims of local residents on foreigners and of foreigners on local residents.

CBOE. Chicago Board Options Exchange.

CBOT. Chicago Board of Trade.

Central bank. The bank acting on behalf of the country's government with the right to issue the country's currency and responsibility to manage the country's money supply, interest rate levels and credit availability. It also manages the level of the country's foreign exchange reserves and the external value of its currency.

Certificate of deposit (CD). A negotiable instrument in bearer form, issued by a bank to certify that a specific sum has been deposited at a stated rate of interest to be repaid on a specific date.

Closed economy. One in which international trade forms a very low percentage of GNP. Such an economy is relatively insensitive to external influences.

CME. Chicago Mercantile Exchange.

Commercial paper. A money market instrument which evidences a money market transaction between two non-financial institutions.

Confirmation. A record of the terms of a foreign exchange or money market transaction sent by each party to the other as evidence of the transaction.

Correspondent bank. A bank located in one geographical area which accepts deposits from a bank in another region and provides services on behalf of the other bank. Internationally banks will maintain accounts with correspondent banks in each financial centre in order to make payments in those countries. Correspondent banks are usually established on a reciprocal basis, the two banks maintaining local currency accounts with each other.

Country limit. An amount of money which a financial institution has established as the maximum it is willing to lend borrowers in a given country regardless of the type of borrower or currencies involved.

Cover. To fix by transactions in the foreign exchange market an exchange rate on funds which will mature or be required at some future date.

Covered interest arbitrage. The process of taking advantage of the disparity between the net accessible interest differential between two currencies and the forward exchange premium or discount on the two currencies against each other.

Crawling peg system. An exchange rate system in which the exchange rate is adjusted every few weeks, usually to reflect prevailing rates of inflation. In between adjustments a fixed rate system prevails.

Credit risk. The likelihood that one party to a transaction may not fulfil its obligation under that transaction.

Cross-currency risk. The risk associated with maintaining opposite net exchange positions in two different currencies as the result of one transaction.

Cross rate. An exchange rate calculated from two other bilateral exchange rates (two different currencies compared with the same third currency).

Currency option. Gives its buyer the right but not the obligation to buy or sell a specific amount of currency at a specific exchange rate on or before a specific date (see Currency option terminology, p. 178).

Currency swap. A simultaneous borrowing and lending operation whereby two parties sell currencies to each other at the spot rate and undertake to reverse the exchange after a fixed term at a fixed exchange rate.

Current account. The net flow of imports and exports in goods and services in the balance of payments between countries.

Demand deposit. See Call money.

Depreciation. A gradual decline in the value of a currency, usually occurring over several days or weeks as a result of market forces of supply and demand. Devaluation, by contrast, is an official government act which produces a susbstantial decline in exchange rates, usually overnight.

Dirty float. A floating exchange rate system in which some government intervention takes place.

Discount. Exchange – When one currency versus another is worth less on a forward basis than it is at the current time.

Interest differential – An instrument issued at current market rates will lose value if rates rise, although the face value remains the same.

Transaction – The practice of taking interest in advance on a foreign facility.

Discount rate. The interest rate used to discount a loan, since the lender can invest the interest received up front to effectively increase the yield on the funds lent.

Domestic money market. A place where local currency is borrowed and deposited by financial institutions and corporations.

Draft. An unconditional order in writing to pay on demand (sight draft) or at a fixed future date (time draft) the amount specified.

Economic exposure. The consequence of movements in exchange rates, which is environmental, occurring irrespective of the base currency. Its effect is an economic rather than a financial risk, though the implications are financial.

ECU. The official unit of the European Monetary System, used as a unit of account for budgetary purposes.

Effective interest rate. The amount of money, expressed as a percentage per annum, actually paid on a loan or deposit. The effective rate may differ from the nominal interest rate, depending on interest payment schedules.

EOE. European Options Exchange.

Eurobond. A bond denominated in an external currency and traded in an external market.

Eurocurrency. A currency which is an asset or a liability in a financial institution outside the home country of the currency – also called external currency or offshore currency.

European Monetary System (**EMS**). An agreement among some European countries to restrict the fluctuations among participating currencies to give a maximum spread – also known as the snake or European basket.

Exchange control. The regulation of the movement and exchange of money by a government or central bank.

Exchange rate. The amount of one currency that can be bought by or sold for a certain amount of another currency.

Exchange rate differential. The difference between two exchange rates in a swap transaction.

Exchange reserves. Total amount of freely convertible foreign currencies held by a country's central bank.

Exchange risk. The variability of a firm's value due to certain exchange rate changes.

Exposure. The amount by which inflows in a given currency are less or greater than outflows in that currency, or vice versa.

Factor. Specialised buyer, at a discount, of a company's receivables.

Fed Funds. Immediately available money deposited with the US Federal Reserve Bank.

Financial futures. Commitment to buy or sell a fixed quantity of a financial instrument at a specified date in the future, at a price generally established through open outcry in a central market place (see Futures market terminology, p. 179).

Fiscal policy. The management of government expenditure and income to accomplish desired economic goals.

Fisher effect. States that the nominal interest differential between two countries should equal the inflation differential between those countries.

Fixed exchange rate system. A system in which the values of various countries' currencies are tied to one major currency, or goal, or the SDR. Fluctuations within a designated band are allowed.

Flat interest rate. A simple percentage interest rate which ignores the element of time.

Float. The money available between the actual receipt of funds and the scheduled payment of those funds.

Floating exchange rate system. A system in which the values of various countries' currencies relative to each other are established by the forces of supply and demand in the market without intervention by the respective governments.

Foreign exchange market. A place where one country's currency can be bought or sold for another country's currency. This market may be a bourse (a physical location) or, more typically, the collection of foreign exchange traders who communicate with each other via telephone and telex.

Forward differential. Annualised percentage difference between the spot and forward rates.

Forward exchange rates. The price of foreign currencies for delivery (on a value date) sometime in the future.

Forward forward. A forward sale against further forward purchase or forward purchase against further forward sale – also applies to money market loans/deposits where a commitment is entered into to borrow/deposit funds in the future for a specified period, based on the interest rate structure prevailing currently.

Free float. An exchange rate system characterised by no government intervention – also known as clean float.

Futures market. A central place or exchange where financial futures are traded by open outcry in a pit (see Futures market terminology, p. 179).

Gap. The period, in foreign exchange transactions, between the maturities for purchase and maturities for sale of each foreign currency (the exchange); in money market transactions, the period between the maturities of loans and maturities of deposits (money market gap).

Hard currency. The currency of a country with large exchange reserves and a surplus in its balance of payments. Exchange of such currency would likely be stable or a candidate for revaluation.

Hedge. To enter into a forward contract in order to protect the home currency value of foreign-currency-denominated assets or liabilities.

Inflation. Price increase for the same goods and services – the effect of competitiveness of a country within world markets.

Interest period. The period for which an interest rate is fixed.

Interest rate. The amount, expressed as a per annum percentage, of money charged for allowing another party the use of it.

Interest rate differential. The difference between the interest rates of two different currencies – also the swap rate between two currencies expressed as a per annum percentage premium or discount.

Interest withholding tax. The amount of money which in some countries is withheld by the local banks, on behalf of the government, from any interest paid to foreigners.

International Monetary Fund (**IMF**). An international organisation created under the Bretton Woods Agreement. Its resources are received from member countries on a quota system and are used to help countries with temporary balance of payments difficulties.

Intervention. The acts of the central bank designed to influence the foreign exchange rate of its currency. The bank uses its reserves to buy its currency if it is under too much downward pressure or to sell it if it is under too much upward pressure.

Lag. To delay payment of a financial obligation.

Lead. To prepay a financial obligation.

Leading and lagging. Accelerating and delaying international payments by modifying credit terms, normally on trade between affiliates, to take advantage of potential devaluations or revaluations of soft or hard currencies respectively.

Letter of credit. A letter addressed to the seller, written and signed by a bank acting on behalf of the buyer, in which the bank promises to honour drafts drawn on itself if the seller conforms to the specific conditions in the letter.

LIFFE. London International Financial Futures Exchange.

Liquidity risk. The chance that it may be impossible to meet financial obligations without delay.

London Interbank Offered Rate (**LIBOR**). The interest rate at which prime banks offer funds to other prime banks in London for specific periods of time.

Long. To have greater inflows than outflows for a given currency. In foreign exchange operations, long positions arise when the amount purchased of the given currency is greater than the amount sold. In money market operations, the long position arises from investing a given currency for a shorter period of time than it is borrowed.

Managed float. See Dirty float.

Monetary policy. The management of several tools at the disposal of a central bank in order to achieve desired economic goals. The tools of monetary policy include control of reserve requirements, the discount rate and open market operations.

Money market. A place where funds can be borrowed or deposited.

Money market instrument. Negotiable instrument which shows someone's obligation to pay a certain amount on a specific date, usually within a year.

Money supply. The currency in circulation plus demand deposits and time deposits; each government has its own broad definition of the money supply categories it monitors.

Multicurrency clause. This gives the borrower the right to switch from borrowing one currency to another on a loan rollover date.

Near money. Instruments which, while not actually cash, are themselves readily exchangeable into cash; e.g. money market instruments.

Net accessible interest differential. The difference between the interest rates which can actually be obtained on two currencies. This difference is usually the basis of the swap rate between the two currencies and is derived from external rather than domestic interest rates. These external rates, or Euro rates, are free from reserve requirements (which would increase the interest rate) and from exchange controls (which would limit access to the money).

Net exchange position. An imbalance between all the assets and purchases of a currency and all the liabilities and sales of the currency; this is not affected by maturity dates.

Nominal exchange rate. The actual spot rate.

Nominal interest rate. The interest rate stated as a percentage of the face value of an instrument.

Non-base. See Base.

Notice money. Funds placed with or borrowed from a financial institution without a fixed maturity but requiring a specific number of days' notice for movements on the account.

Offer rate. The price at which the quoting party is prepared to sell or lend currency.

Official reserves. See Exchange reserves.

Offshore finance subsidiary. A wholly owned affiliate incorporated overseas, usually in a tax haven country, whose function is to issue securities abroad for use in the parent's domestic or foreign funding.

Open economy. One in which international trade forms a high percentage of GNP. Such an economy is sensitive to external influences.

Open market operations. The actions of a central bank behaving like a commercial bank in its local money market.

Open position. The long or short position at any time during which an exchange risk is run.

Operating exposure. Degree to which an exchange rate change, in combination with price changes, will alter a company's future operating cash flows.

Option exchange contract. A contract for foreign exchange without a fixed maturity date. In this type of contract, a period of time is stated during which the person who has the option can choose any day for liquidation and settlement of contract. The contract must state which party has the option (the buyer or the seller) and is usually employed when the date on which the foreign exchange will be needed or will be available is not precisely known.

Option market. A place where currency option contracts are traded (see Currency option terminology, p. 178).

Outright rate. Actual forward exchange rate.

Overbought. Position of a trader who has bought a larger amount of currency than he has sold.

Overnight position. A foreign exchange or money market position outstanding overnight; can be risky, therefore open overnight positions tend to be transferred to the next financial centre in the next time zone to be managed.

Oversold. Position of a trader who has a sold a larger amount of currency than he has bought.

Par. When the forward exchange rate is the same as the spot exchange rate.

PHLX. Philadelphia Stock Exchange.

Pip. Thousandth part of a unit.

Political risk. See Sovereign risk.

Pooling. Transfer of excess affiliate cash into a central account (pool) usually located in a low-tax nation, where funds can be managed centrally.

Position. A situation created through foreign exchange contracts (exchange position) or interest differential contracts (deposit market position) in which changes in interest rates or exchange rates could create profits or losses for the trader.

Premium. The amount, usually expressed as a per annum percentage rate (a swap rate), by which the forward exchange rate of one currency against another is stronger than the spot exchange rate between the two currencies.

Price quotation. See Reciprocal rate.

Purchasing power parity. The notion that the ratio between domestic and foreign price levels should equal the equilibrium exchange rate between domestic and foreign currencies.

Rate risk. In the deposit market, the chance that interest rates may rise when the trader has a short position or vice versa. Similarly, in the exchange rate market the chance that the spot rate may rise when the trader has a net oversold position (a short position) and vice versa.

Real exchange rate. The spot rate adjusted for relative price level changes since the base period.

Reciprocal rate. The price of one currency in terms of a second currency when the price of the second currency is given in terms of the first.

Repurchase agreement. A contract in which the seller of an asset agrees to buy back the asset on a future date.

Reserve requirement. Amount of money which commercial banks are required to keep on deposit with a central bank.

SFE. Sydney Futures Exchange.

Short. In foreign exchange operations, when the amount of a given currency sold is greater than the amount bought. In money market transactions, when funds borrowed are for a shorter period than those invested.

Simex. Singapore International Monetary Exchange.

Soft currency. The currency of a country with low exchange reserves and a deficit in the balance of payments; as such, considered as an object for devaluation.

Sovereign risk. The risk that a government of a country may interfere with the repayment of debt.

Special Drawing Rights (SDR). International paper money created and distributed by the IMF to governments in quantities and at times dictated by special agreements. The value of an SDR is determined by the weighted value of a basket of major currencies.

Spot rate. The price of foreign currencies for delivery in two business days' time.

Spread. The difference between the bid rate and offer rate in an exchange rate quote or an interest quote.

Square. The absence of a position.

Swap. The purchase of one currency against another for one maturity date and a simultaneous reversal of that exchange contract for a different maturity.

Swap rate. The difference between the spot exchange rate of a given currency and its forward exchange rate.

Technical rally. Price movement attributed to conditions developing from within the market itself.

Tight market. One in which investors are reluctant to commit funds, thus causing a shortage of liquidity.

Time deposit. The placement of funds with a financial institution for a fixed period of time, usually longer than a month.

Trade acceptance. A draft accepted by a commercial enterprise.

Trade accounts. Those elements of the balance of payments which reflect money spent abroad by residents on goods and services and the money spent in the country by foreigners on goods and services.

Trade draft. A draft addressed to a commercial enterprise.

Transaction exposure. The effect of currency movements on current cash flows, and impact on future flows, between the time of transaction initiation and completion.

Transfer price. The price at which one unit of a firm sells goods or services to an affiliated unit.

Translation exposure. The effect of currency movements on assets and liabilities in one or more currencies and of consolidating them into a base currency at the end of each financial period.

Treasury bills. The obligations of a country's treasury department.

Two-way rate. An exchange rate or interest rate quotation which contains both a bid and an offer rate.

Value or value date. The date on which a financial transaction is to be settled – also known as the maturity date.

Currency option/futures market terminology

CURRENCY OPTION

American option. An option which may be exercised at any time until the expiration date (also known as a spot option).

At the money. An option with a rate equal to the current spot rate.

Call option. The right (not the obligation) to buy foreign currency.

European option. An option which can be exercised only on the expiration date (also known as a forward option).

Exercise. Conversion of the option into its underlying spot or forward contract.

Expiration date. Last business day on which the option can be exercised, which is two business days before the value date.

Holder. Party which has the option to buy (or sell) the currency.

In the money. An option with a rate better than the current spot rate, for the option holder.

Intrinsic value. The value to the holder of exercising the option immediately, i.e. the difference between the strike price and market price (spot or forward).

Out the money. An option with a rate worse than the current spot rate, for the option holder.

Premium. Price of the option, i.e. the amount paid by the holder to the writer for the option contract.

Put option. The right (not the obligation) to sell foreign currency.

Strike price or **exercise rate.** Fixed rate at which the currency can be exercised (bought or sold) during the option period.

Time value. The value to the holder representing the difference between the premium and the intrinsic value; i.e. the time left until expiration.

Value date. Last day on which currency may be delivered.

Writer. Party giving the right to buy (or sell) a currency, in return for a premium.

FUTURES MARKET

At the market. An order to buy or sell at the best price obtainable at the time the order is received.

Basis. The difference between the cash price for a financial instrument and the price of the particular futures contract relating to that price.

Cash market. The underlying currency or money market in which deals are carried out in instruments to which futures contracts relate.

Clearing-house. Organisation which acts as a buyer to the seller and seller to the buyer, giving the market one settlement counterparty for all trades. It is responsible for processing documentation and ensuring the smooth operation of the market financially by calling for margin payments, etc.

Clearing members. The only organisations to have access to the clearing-house for the purpose of matching trades effected on their clients' behalf.

Close. End of a trading session; sometimes refers to the closing price, i.e. the last price quoted.

Commission. One-off fee charged by a broker to a customer when a position is liquidated by a delivery or offset.

Contract. Refers to a specific future instrument. Each exchange details the contracts that are traded on the exchange, and their terms and conditions.

Contract grade. That grade of financial instrument which has been officially approved by the exchange as deliverable in settlement of a futures contract.

Contract month. The month in which the contract is deliverable.

Cover. The purchase or sale of contracts to offset previous positions.

Delivery. Actual settlement of the instrument by the seller to the clearing-house, then to the buyer.

Delivery price. The settlement price, fixed by the clearing-house at which deliveries on futures are invoiced.

Discount. The amount by which the futures price is below that of the cash market.

Hedge. The purchase or sale of futures contracts opposite to the position held in the cash market.

ICCH. International Commodities Clearing House.

Limit (up or down). The maximum amount the contract price can change during one trading session, as fixed by the exchange.

Long hedge. Hedge against a fall in interest rates.

Maintenance margin (variation margin). Amount required in cash to restore the original margin position.

Margin (initial margin). The cash amount deposited with the broker to guarantee performance of the contract.

Margin call. Demand for funds for margin maintenance following an adverse price movement.

Mark to market. Procedure by which all contracts are revalued on a daily basis at the closing price. Position profits and losses are calculated and margin calls initiated.

Minimum price fluctuation (tick). Smallest price movement permitted by the exchange in a given contract.

Open contracts. Contracts which have been bought and sold without the transaction being completed by subsequent sale or purchase.

Open interest. Number of open futures contracts.

Premium. The excess of a futures price over the comparable cash market price.

Scalp. To trade for small gains.

Short hedge. Hedge against a rise in interest rates.

Stop-loss order. An order which becomes a market order when 'stop' level is reached. Its purpose is to limit losses.

Straddle. The simultaneous purchase and sale of futures contracts for the same type of interest rate or currency futures, but for delivery in different months.

Volume. Number of contracts traded in a particular future on any one day.

Index